Table of Contents

Introduction

A Ketogenic diet is the best thing that could ever happen to you! Trust us! Millions of people all around the world have already discovered this special lifestyle and they all recommend it!

A Ketogenic diet will change you forever! It brings you so many health benefits and it helps you look and feel amazing!

This diet is easy to follow and it will soon show all its positive effects.

If you decided to start a Ketogenic diet, you should probably keep in mind some simple rules you need to follow!

You can consume a lot of veggies and fruits, organic meat, poultry, fish and seafood.

You can also consume nuts and seeds, cheese and healthy oils.

On the other hand, if you are on a Ketogenic diet you are not allowed to eat beans, grains, sugar and artificial ingredients!

Come on, it's not that complicated!

So, have you started a Ketogenic diet yet?

Perfect! Then, all you need now is to learn how to make the best Ketogenic dishes!

We've checked thousands of Ketogenic recipes and we find them all amazing but we thought you could be interested in discovering a new way to make keto meals.

We are talking about cooking keto meals using one of the best kitchen appliances ever: an instant pot!

We won't tell you more! It's time for you to discover the best keto dishes made in your instant pot!

Enjoy!

Ketogenic Instant Pot Main Dish Recipes

Cauliflower Soup

Preparation time: 10 minutes
Cooking time: 10 minutes
Servings: 4

Ingredients:

- 2 tablespoons olive oil
- 1 small yellow onion, chopped
- 1 cauliflower head, florets separated and chopped
- 3 cups chicken stock
- 1 teaspoon garlic powder
- 4 ounces cream cheese, cubed
- A pinch of salt and black pepper
- 1 cup cheddar cheese, shredded
- ½ cup coconut milk

Directions:

Set your instant pot on sauté mode, add oil, heat it up, add onion, stir and cook for 3 minutes. Add cauliflower, stir and cook for 1 minute more. Add stock, mil and garlic powder, stir, cover and cook on High for 6 minutes. Add cream cheese and pulse everything using an immersion blender. Add cheddar cheese, stir soup, ladle into bowls and serve. Enjoy!

Nutrition: calories 261, fat 4, fiber 4, carbs 7, protein 8

Chicken and Delicious Sauce

Preparation time: 1 hour and 10 minutes
Cooking time: 20 minutes
Servings: 4

Ingredients:

- 2 chicken breasts, skinless, boneless and chopped
- 1 tablespoon lemon juice
- 1 cup Greek yogurt
- 1 tablespoon garam masala
- ¼ teaspoon ginger, grated
- A pinch of salt and black pepper

For the sauce:

- 4 teaspoons garam masala
- 4 garlic cloves, minced
- 15 ounces canned tomato sauce
- ½ teaspoon paprika
- ½ teaspoon turmeric
- ¼ teaspoon cayenne

Directions:

In a bowl, mix chicken with lemon juice, yogurt, 1 tablespoon garam masala, ginger, salt and pepper, toss well and leave aside in the fridge for 1 hour. Set your instant pot on sauté mode, add chicken, stir and cook for 5 minutes. Add 4 teaspoons garam masala, garlic, tomato sauce, paprika, turmeric and cayenne, stir, cover the pot and cook on High for 10 minutes. Divide between plates and serve. Enjoy!

Nutrition: calories 452, fat 4, fiber 7, carbs 9, protein 12

Different Lasagna

Preparation time: 10 minutes
Cooking time: 25 minutes
Servings: 8

Ingredients:

- 2 garlic cloves, minced
- 1 pound beef, ground
- 1 yellow onion, chopped
- 1 egg

- ½ cup parmesan cheese, grated
- 1 and ½ cups ricotta cheese
- 20 ounces keto marinara sauce
- 8 ounces mozzarella, sliced

Directions:

Set your instant pot on sauté mode, add onion, garlic and beef, stir and sauté for 5 minutes. Add marinara sauce, stir and transfer half of this mix to a bowl. In another bowl, mix ricotta with parmesan and egg and whisk well. Add half of the mozzarella to your instant pot and spread. Add half of the ricotta mix and spread. Add the remaining beef and marinara mix, the rest of the mozzarella and the rest of the ricotta mix. Cover this with some tin foil, cover the pot and cook on High for 10 minutes. Slice lasagna, divide between plates and serve. Enjoy!

Nutrition: calories 339, fat 4, fiber 2, carbs 8, protein 36

Delicious Pork Chops

Preparation time: 10 minutes
Cooking time: 10 minutes
Servings: 4

Ingredients:

- 4 pork chops, boneless
- 1 tablespoon olive oil
- 3 tablespoons ghee, melted

- 1 cup chicken stock
- A pinch of salt and black pepper
- ¼ teaspoon sweet paprika

Directions:

Set your instant pot on sauté mode, add the oil, heat it up, add pork chops and brown for a few minutes on each side. Add ghee, salt, pepper, paprika and stock, stir, cover pot and cook on High for 5 minutes. Serve your pork chops with a keto side salad. Enjoy!

Nutrition: calories 362, fat 4, fiber 8, carbs 10, protein 19

Chili Bowl

Preparation time: 10 minutes
Cooking time: 15 minutes
Servings: 4

Ingredients:
- 2 pounds beef steak strips, cubed
- 1 teaspoon garlic, minced
- 1 tablespoon water
- 2 teaspoon lime juice
- ½ teaspoon chili powder
- 1 tablespoon olive oil
- A pinch of salt and black pepper
- 3 avocados, pitted, peeled and cubed

Directions:
Set your instant pot on sauté mode, add the oil, heat it up, add garlic, stir and cook for 1 minute. Add beef, stir and brown for 3 minutes more. Add water, lime juice, chili powder, salt and pepper, stir, cover the pot and cook on High for 10 minutes. Set the pot on sauté mode again, cook beef mix for a couple more minutes, divide into bowls and serve with avocados on top. Enjoy!

Nutrition: calories 300, fat 5, fiber 4, carbs 8, protein 17

Chicken and Squash Spaghetti

Preparation time: 10 minutes
Cooking time: 20 minutes
Servings: 4

Ingredients:
- 1 spaghetti squash, halved and seedless
- 1 cup water
- 1 cup keto marinara sauce
- 1 pound chicken, cooked and cubed
- 16 ounces mozzarella cheese, shredded

Directions:
Put 1 cup water in your instant pot, add the trivet, add squash, cover and cook on High for 20 minutes. Shred squash into spaghetti and transfer to a heatproof bowl. Add marinara sauce, chicken and mozzarella, toss, introduce in preheated broiler and cook for a few minutes. Divide into bowls and serve. Enjoy!

Nutrition: calories 329, fat 6, fiber 6, carbs 9, protein 10

Easy Pork Roast

Preparation time: 10 minutes
Cooking time: 45 minutes
Servings: 12

Ingredients:
- ½ cup beef stock
- 1 tablespoon olive oil
- ¼ cup keto Jamaican spice mix
- 4 pounds pork shoulder

Directions:

In a bowl, mix pork with oil and spice mix and rub well. Set your instant pot on sauté mode, add pork and brown for a few minutes on each side. Add stock, cover pot and cook pork shoulder on High for 40 minutes. Slice roast and serve. Enjoy!

Nutrition: calories 400, fat 6, fiber 7, carbs 10, protein 16

Broccoli Soup

Preparation time: 10 minutes
Cooking time: 10 minutes
Servings: 4

Ingredients:
- 1 broccoli head, florets separated and roughly chopped
- 4 cups chicken stock
- A pinch of salt and white pepper
- ¼ teaspoon garlic powder
- 1 cup carrots, chopped
- 2 tablespoons ghee, melted
- 1 yellow onion, chopped
- 2 cups cheddar cheese, shredded
- 1 cup coconut cream

Directions:

Set your instant pot on sauté mode, add ghee, heat it up, add onion, stir and cook for 2-3 minutes. Add carrots, broccoli, stock, garlic powder, salt and pepper, stir, cover and cook on High for 5 minutes. Add cream and cheese, stir, ladle into bowls and serve. Enjoy!

Nutrition: calories 320, fat 6, fiber 7, carbs 9, protein 12

Pork Chops and Gravy

Preparation time: 10 minutes
Cooking time: 25 minutes
Servings: 4

Ingredients:

- 3 bacon slices, chopped
- 3 garlic cloves, minced
- 1 tablespoon olive oil
- 1 small yellow onion, chopped
- 8 ounces mushrooms, sliced
- 4 pork chops, bone in
- 1 cup beef stock
- 1 teaspoon garlic powder
- 1 thyme sprigs, chopped
- 10 ounces cream of mushrooms
- 1 tablespoon parsley, chopped

Directions:

Set your instant pot on sauté mode, add oil, heat it up, add bacon, stir and cook for 2 minutes. Add garlic, onion and mushrooms, stir and cook for 3 minutes more. Add pork chops, garlic powder, stock and thyme, stir, cover and cook on High for 20 minutes. Add cream of mushrooms, stir, set the pot on simmer mode, cook for a few minutes and divide everything between plates. Sprinkle parsley on top and serve. Enjoy!

Nutrition: calories 400, fat 8, fiber 7, carbs 12, protein 17

Pork Bowls

Preparation time: 10 minutes
Cooking time: 45 minutes
Servings: 4

Ingredients:

- 2 pounds pork sirloin roast, cut into thick slices
- A pinch of salt and black pepper
- 2 teaspoons garlic powder
- 2 teaspoons cumin, ground
- 1 tablespoon olive oil
- 16 ounces keto green chili tomatillo salsa

Directions:

In a bowl, mix pork with cumin, salt, pepper and garlic powder and rub well. Set your instant pot on sauté mode, add the oil heat it up, add pork and brown on all sides. Add salsa, toss a bit, cover and cook on High for 45 minutes. Divide between plates and serve hot. Enjoy!

Nutrition: calories 400, fat 7, fiber 6, carbs 10, protein 14

Beef Meatloaf

Preparation time: 10 minutes
Cooking time: 20 minutes
Servings: 4

Ingredients:

- 2 pounds beef, ground
- ¼ cup parmesan, grated
- ¼ cup yellow onion, chopped
- 1 egg, whisked
- A pinch of salt and black pepper
- 1 tablespoon garlic, minced
- ½ teaspoon thyme, dried
- 1 tablespoon olive oil
- 1 yellow onion, chopped
- 1 cup keto ketchup
- ½ cup beef stock

Directions:

In a bowl, mix beef with cheese, ¼ cup onion, egg, thyme, salt and pepper and stir really well. Set your instant pot on sauté mode, add the oil, heat it up, and 1 yellow onion, stir and cook for 4 minutes. Add stock and ketchup, stir and cook for 1 minute more. Shape a round meatloaf out of the beef mix, add it to the pot, cover and cook on High for 15 minutes. Divide meatloaf on plates, drizzle the sauce from the pot all over and serve. Enjoy!

Nutrition: calories 363, fat 6, fiber 3, carbs 8, protein 14

Pork and Veggies

Preparation time: 10 minutes
Cooking time: 15 minutes
Servings: 6

Ingredients:

- 1 pound pork, ground
- 1 tablespoon olive oil
- ½ cup yellow onion, chopped
- 1 cup red bell peppers, chopped
- 2 garlic cloves, minced
- ½ cup parmesan, grated
- 4 cups baby spinach

Directions:

Set your instant pot on sauté mode, add the oil, heat it up, add pork, stir and brown for a couple of minutes. Add garlic, onion, spinach and bell peppers, stir, cover and cook on High for 3 minutes. Divide this into bowls, sprinkle cheese on top and serve. Enjoy!

Nutrition: calories 241, fat 10, fiber 2, carbs 5, protein 15

Chicken and Tasty Cauliflower Rice

Preparation time: 10 minutes
Cooking time: 28 minutes
Servings: 6

Ingredients:

- 3 bacon slices, chopped
- 3 carrots, chopped
- 3 pounds chicken thighs, boneless and skinless
- 1 rhubarb stalk, chopped
- 2 bay leaves
- ¼ cup red wine vinegar
- 4 garlic cloves, minced
- A pinch of salt and black pepper
- ¼ cup olive oil
- 1 tablespoon garlic powder
- 1 tablespoon Italian seasoning
- 24 ounces cauliflower rice
- 1 teaspoon turmeric powder
- 1 cup beef stock

Directions:

Set your instant pot on sauté mode, add bacon, carrots, onion, rhubarb and garlic, stir and cook for 8 minutes. Add chicken, stir and cook for 1 minute more. Add oil, vinegar, turmeric, Italian seasoning, garlic powder and bay leaves, stir, cover and cook on High for 20 minutes. Add cauliflower rice and stock, stir, cover and cook on Low for 3 minutes more. Divide into bowls and serve. Enjoy!

Nutrition: calories 310, fat 6, fiber 3, carbs 6, protein 10

Chicken Curry

Preparation time: 10 minutes
Cooking time: 30 minutes
Servings: 4

Ingredients:

- 3 tomatoes, chopped
- 2 pounds chicken thighs, skinless, boneless and cubed
- 2 tablespoons olive oil
- 1 cup chicken stock
- 14 ounces canned coconut milk
- 2 garlic cloves, minced
- 1 cup white onion, chopped
- 3 red chilies, chopped
- 1 tablespoon water
- 1 tablespoon ginger, grated
- 2 teaspoons coriander, ground
- 1 teaspoon cinnamon, ground
- 1 teaspoon turmeric, ground
- 1 teaspoon cumin, ground
- 1 teaspoon fennel seeds, ground
- 1 tablespoon lime juice
- Salt and black pepper

Directions:

In your food processor, mix white onion with garlic, chilies, water, ginger, coriander, cinnamon, turmeric, cumin, fennel and black pepper, blend until you obtain a paste and transfer to a bowl. Set your instant pot on sauté mode, add the oil, heat it up, add blended paste, stir and cook for 30 seconds. Add chicken, tomatoes and stock, stir, cover pot and cook on High for 15 minutes. Add coconut milk, stir, cover pot again and cook on High for 7 minutes more. Add lime juice, salt and pepper, stir, divide into bowls and serve. Enjoy!

Nutrition: calories 430, fat 16, fiber 4, carbs 7, protein 38

Shrimp and Zucchini Spaghetti

Preparation time: 10 minutes
Cooking time: 6 minutes
Servings: 4

Ingredients:

- 12 ounces zucchini, cut with a spiralizer
- 2 tablespoons veggie stock
- 2 tablespoons ghee
- 2 tablespoons olive oil
- Salt and black pepper to the taste
- 4 garlic cloves, minced
- 1 pound shrimp, raw, peeled and deveined
- Juice of ½ lemon
- ½ teaspoon sweet paprika
- A handful basil, chopped

Directions:

Set your instant pot on sauté mode, add ghee and olive oil, heat them up, add garlic, stir and cook for 1 minute. Add shrimp, stock and lemon juice and cook for 1 minute more. Add zucchini pasta, salt, pepper and paprika, stir, cover pot and cook on High for 3 minutes more. Divide this into bowls, sprinkle basil on top and serve. Enjoy!

Nutrition: calories 300, fat 20, fiber 6, carbs 3, protein 30

Fish and Carrot Soup

Preparation time: 10 minutes
Cooking time: 20 minutes
Servings: 4

Ingredients:

- 1 yellow onion, chopped
- 12 cups chicken stock
- 1 pound carrots, sliced
- 1 tablespoon coconut oil
- Salt and black pepper to the taste
- 2 tablespoons ginger, minced
- 1 cup water
- 1 pound halibut, skinless, boneless and cut into medium chunks

Directions:

Set your instant pot on sauté mode, add oil, heat it up, add onion, stir and cook for 4 minutes. Add water, stock, ginger and carrots, stir, cover and cook on High for 8 minutes. Blend soup using an immersion blender, add halibut pieces, salt and pepper, stir a bit, cover pot and cook on High for 6 minutes. Ladle into bowls and serve hot. Enjoy!

Nutrition: calories 170, fat 6, fiber 2, carbs 6, protein 12

Trout Fillet and Sauce

Preparation time: 10 minutes
Cooking time: 6 minutes
Servings: 4

Ingredients:

- 4 trout fillets, boneless
- Salt and black pepper to the taste
- 3 teaspoons lemon zest, grated
- 3 tablespoons chives, chopped
- 6 tablespoons ghee
- 2 tablespoons olive oil
- 2 teaspoons lemon juice

Directions:

Set your instant pot on sauté mode, add oil and ghee, heat them up, and fish, lemon zest, lemon juice, salt and pepper, stir, cover and cook on Low for 4 minutes. Divide fish and ghee sauce on plates, sprinkle chives on top and serve. Enjoy!

Nutrition: calories 320, fat 6, fiber 1, carbs 4, protein 18

Shrimp and Mushrooms

Preparation time: 10 minutes
Cooking time: 20 minutes
Servings: 4

Ingredients:

- 8 ounces mushrooms, chopped
- 1 pound shrimp, peeled and deveined
- 1 yellow onion, chopped
- 1 asparagus bunch, cut into medium pieces
- Salt and black pepper to the taste
- 1 spaghetti squash, cut into halves
- 2 tablespoons olive oil
- 2 teaspoons Italian seasoning
- 1 teaspoon red pepper flakes, crushed
- ¼ cup ghee
- 1 cup parmesan cheese, grated
- 2 garlic cloves, minced
- 1 cup coconut cream
- 2 cups water

Directions:

Put the water in your instant pot, add steamer basket, add spaghetti halves, cover, cook on High for 10 minutes, scoop insides and transfer them to a bowl. Add asparagus to the steamer basket, cover pot again, cook on High for 3 minutes, cool it down in a bowl filled with ice water, drain and leave aside. Clean your instant pot, set it on sauté mode, add oil and ghee, heat it up, add mushrooms and onion, stir and cook for 3-4 minutes. Add pepper flakes, Italian seasoning, salt, pepper, squash and asparagus, stir and cook for a few minutes more. Add coconut cream, parmesan, garlic and shrimp, cover pot and cook on High for 4 minutes. Divide everything between plates and serve. Enjoy!

Nutrition: calories 465, fat 6, fiber 2, carbs 5, protein 10

Lemon and Garlic Shrimp

Preparation time: 10 minutes
Cooking time: 3 minutes
Servings: 4

Ingredients:

- 2 tablespoons olive oil
- 1 tablespoon ghee
- 1 pound shrimp, peeled and deveined
- 2 tablespoons lemon juice
- 2 tablespoons garlic, minced
- 1 tablespoon lemon zest
- Salt and black pepper to the taste

Directions:

Set your instant pot on sauté mode, add oil and ghee, heat them up, add garlic, shrimp, lemon juice, lemon zest, salt and pepper, stir, cover and cook on High for 3 minutes. Divide everything between plates and serve. Enjoy!

Nutrition: calories 159, fat 1, fiber 3, carbs 5, protein 5

Haddock and Mayonnaise

Preparation time: 10 minutes
Cooking time: 7 minutes
Servings: 4

Ingredients:

- 1 pound haddock
- 2 tablespoons mayonnaise
- 3 teaspoons veggie stock
- 2 tablespoons lemon juice
- Salt and black pepper to the taste
- 1 teaspoon dill, chopped
- A drizzle of olive oil
- ¼ teaspoon old bay seasoning

Directions:

In your instant pot, mix haddock with stock, lemon juice, mayo, salt, pepper, dill, oil and old bay seasoning, toss a bit, cover and cook on High for 7 minutes. Divide everything between plates and serve. Enjoy!

Nutrition: calories 164, fat 12, fiber 1, carbs 6, protein 14

Chicken and Mushrooms

Preparation time: 10 minutes
Cooking time: 15 minutes
Servings: 4

Ingredients:
- 4 chicken thighs
- 2 cups mushrooms, sliced
- ¼ cup ghee
- Salt and black pepper to the taste
- ½ teaspoon onion powder
- ½ teaspoon garlic powder
- ½ cup water
- 1 teaspoon Dijon mustard
- 1 tablespoon tarragon, chopped

Directions:
Set your instant pot on sauté mode, add ghee, melt it, add chicken, salt, pepper, onion powder and garlic powder, stir, cook for 2 minutes on each side and transfer to a bowl. Add mushrooms to your instant pot, stir and sauté them for 2 minutes more. Return chicken to the pot, also add mustard and water, stir well, cover and cook on High for 10 minutes. Add tarragon, stir, divide between plates and serve right away. Enjoy!

Nutrition: calories 263, fat 16, fiber 4, carbs 6, protein 18

Chicken and Salsa

Preparation time: 10 minutes
Cooking time: 17 minutes
Servings: 6

Ingredients:
- 6 chicken breasts, skinless and boneless
- 2 cups jarred keto salsa
- Salt and black pepper to the taste
- 1 cup cheddar cheese, shredded
- A drizzle of olive oil

Directions:
Set your instant pot on sauté mode, add a drizzle of oil, heat it up, add chicken, stir and cook for 2 minutes on each side. Add salsa, stir, cover and cook on High for 7 minutes. Spread cheese all over, cover pot again and cook on High for 3 minutes more. Divide between plates and serve right away. Enjoy!

Nutrition: calories 220, fat 7, fiber 2, carbs 6, protein 12

Salsa Chicken Soup

Preparation time: 10 minutes
Cooking time: 15 minutes
Servings: 6

Ingredients:

- 1 and ½ pounds chicken tights, skinless, boneless and cubed
- 15 ounces chicken stock
- 15 ounces canned keto chunky salsa
- 8 ounces Monterey jack cheese, shredded

Directions:

In your instant pot, mix chicken with stock, salsa and cheese, stir, cover and cook on High for 15 minutes. Stir soup, ladle into bowls and serve. Enjoy!

Nutrition: calories 270, fat 16, fiber 3, carbs 5, protein 22

Hot Beef Stew

Preparation time: 10 minutes
Cooking time: 8 hours
Servings: 4

Ingredients:

- 1 yellow onion, chopped
- 2 and ½ pounds beef, ground
- 15 ounces canned tomatoes and green chilies, chopped
- 6 ounces tomato paste
- 2 jalapenos, chopped
- 4 tablespoons garlic, minced
- 3 celery ribs, chopped
- 2 tablespoons coconut aminos
- 4 tablespoons chili powder
- Salt and black pepper to the taste
- A pinch of cayenne pepper
- 1 bay leaf
- 2 tablespoons cumin, ground
- 1 teaspoon oregano, dried
- 1 teaspoon onion powder
- 1 teaspoon garlic powder

Directions:

Set your instant pot on sauté mode, add beef, onion, garlic, salt and pepper, stir and cook for 3-4 minutes. Add celery, jalapenos, tomatoes and chilies mix, tomato paste, tomatoes, aminos, cayenne, cumin, onion powder, garlic powder, bay leaf and oregano, stir, cover and cook on High for 15 minutes. Discard bay leaf, divide stew among bowls and serve. Enjoy!

Nutrition: calories 327, fat 7, fiber 2, carbs 5, protein 22

Leg of Lamb and Spinach Salad

Preparation time: 10 minutes
Cooking time: 40 minutes
Servings: 4

Ingredients:
- 1 tablespoon olive oil
- 2 garlic cloves, minced
- 2 cups veggie stock
- 3 pounds leg of lamb, bone discarded and butterflied

- Salt and black pepper to the taste
- 1 teaspoon cumin, ground
- ¼ teaspoon thyme, dried

For the salad:
- 4 ounces feta cheese, crumbled
- ½ cup pecans, toasted
- 2 cups spinach

- 1 and ½ tablespoons lemon juice
- ¼ cup olive oil
- 1 cup mint, chopped

Directions:

Rub lamb with salt, pepper, 1 tablespoon oil, thyme, cumin and garlic. Add the stock to your instant pot, add leg of lamb, cover and cook on High for 40 minutes. Leave leg of lamb aside to cool down, slice and divide between plates. Meanwhile, in a bowl, mix spinach with mint, feta cheese, ¼ cup olive oil, lemon juice, pecans, salt and pepper, toss and divide next to lamb slices. Serve right away. Enjoy!

Nutrition: calories 234, fat 20, fiber 3, carbs 5, protein 12

Lamb Stew

Preparation time: 10 minutes
Cooking time: 20 minutes
Servings: 4

Ingredients:
- 1 yellow onion, chopped
- 2 pounds lamb meat, cubed
- 2 tablespoons ghee
- 3 carrots, chopped
- 2 cups beef stock

- 1 tomato, chopped
- 1 garlic clove, minced
- Salt and black pepper to the taste
- 2 rosemary sprigs, chopped
- 1 teaspoon thyme, chopped

Directions:

Set your instant pot on sauté mode, add ghee, heat it up, add lamb meat and brown for 2 minutes on all sides. Add onion, stir and cook for 1 minute more. Add carrots, tomato, garlic, thyme, rosemary, salt, pepper and stock, stir, cover and cook on High for 15 minutes. Divide into bowls and serve. Enjoy!

Nutrition: calories 260, fat 12, fiber 6, carbs 10, protein 36

Beef and Mushroom Stew

Preparation time: 10 minutes
Cooking time: 20 minutes
Servings: 5

Ingredients:

- 2 pounds beef chuck roast, cubed
- 1 cup beef stock
- 1 cup water
- 2 yellow onions, chopped
- 15 ounces canned tomatoes, chopped
- 4 carrots, chopped
- Salt and black pepper to the taste
- ½ pound mushrooms, sliced
- 2 celery ribs, chopped
- 1 tablespoon thyme, chopped
- ½ teaspoon mustard powder
- 2 tablespoons coconut flour

Directions:

Set your instant pot on sauté mode, add beef, stir and brown for 2 minutes on each side. Add tomatoes, mushrooms, onions, carrots, celery, salt, pepper mustard, stock, flour and thyme, stir, cover and cook on High for 15 minutes. Divide into bowls and serve. Enjoy!

Nutrition: calories 275, fat 7, fiber 4, carbs 7, protein 28

Pomegranate and Walnuts Chicken

Preparation time: 10 minutes
Cooking time: 17 minutes
Servings: 6

Ingredients:

- 12 chicken thighs
- 2 cups walnuts, toasted and chopped
- Salt and black pepper to the taste
- 3 tablespoons olive oil
- 1 yellow onion, chopped
- Juice of ½ lemon
- ¼ teaspoon cardamom, ground
- ½ teaspoon cinnamon, ground
- 1 cup pomegranate molasses
- 2 tablespoons stevia

Directions:

Put walnuts in your food processor, blend and transfer to a bowl. Set your instant pot on sauté mode, add 2 tablespoons oil, heat it up, add chicken, salt and pepper, brown for a couple of minutes on each side and transfer to a bowl. Add the rest of the oil to your instant pot, heat it up, add onion, stir and cook for 3 minutes. Add cardamom, cinnamon, walnuts, pomegranate molasses, chicken, stevia and lemon juice, stir, cover and cook on High for 10 minutes. Divide everything between plates and serve. Enjoy!

Nutrition: calories 265, fat 6, fiber 6, carbs 14, protein 16

Sausages and Mashed Celeriac

Preparation time: 15 minutes
Cooking time: 15 minutes
Servings: 6

Ingredients:
For the mash
- 2 celeriac, peeled and cut into cubes
- Salt and black pepper to the taste
- 1 teaspoon mustard powder
- 1 tablespoon ghee, melted
- 4 ounces warm coconut milk
- 6 ounces water
- 1 tablespoon cheddar cheese, grated

For the sausages:
- 6 pork sausages
- 2 tablespoons olive oil
- ½ cup keto onion jam
- 2 ounces veggie stock
- 3 ounces water
- Salt and black pepper to the taste

Directions:
Put celeriac cubes in your instant pot, add 6 ounces water, salt and pepper, stir, cover, cook on High for 6 minutes, drain, transfer to a bowl and mash using a potato masher. Add mustard powder, ghee, milk and cheese, stir really well and leave aside for now. Set your instant pot on Sauté mode, add oil, heat it up, add sausages and brown them on all sides. Add onion jam, stock, 3 ounces water, salt and pepper, stir, cover and cook on High for 8 minutes. Divide sausages on plates, add mashed celeriac on the side and serve with some of the cooking juices from the pot drizzled all over. Enjoy!

Nutrition: calories 421, fat 12, fiber 4, carbs 7, protein 15

Seafood Summer Mix

Preparation time: 10 minutes
Cooking time: 15 minutes
Servings: 4

Ingredients:
- 12 shell clams
- 12 mussels
- 1 and ½ pounds shrimp, peeled and deveined
- 1 and ½ pounds fish fillets, cut into medium pieces
- 20 ounces canned tomatoes, chopped
- 5 tablespoons ghee, melted
- 3 garlic cloves, minced
- 2 yellow onions, chopped
- 4 tablespoons parsley, chopped
- 8 ounces clam juice
- 1 and ½ cups veggie stock
- 2 bay leaves
- ½ teaspoon marjoram, dried
- 1 tablespoon basil, dried
- Salt and black pepper to the taste

Directions:
Set your instant pot on Sauté mode, add ghee, heat it up, add onion and garlic, stir and cook for a couple of minutes. Add clam juice, tomatoes, stock, parsley, basil, bay leaves, marjoram, salt and pepper, stir, cover and cook on High for 10 minutes. Add clams and mussels, stir, set the pot on simmer mode and cook for 8 minutes. Add fish and shrimp, stir, cook for 4 minutes, ladle into bowls and serve. Enjoy!

Nutrition: calories 300, fat 10, fiber 7, carbs 10, protein 17

Mexican Chicken Soup

Preparation time: 10 minutes
Cooking time: 30 minutes
Servings: 4

Ingredients:

- 2 chicken breasts, boneless and skinless and cubed
- 1 and ¼ cup jarred keto enchilada sauce
- 3 cups chicken stock
- 16 ounces canned tomatoes, chopped
- 4 ounces canned green chilies, chopped
- Salt and black pepper to the taste
- 2 garlic cloves, minced
- 1 cup white onion, chopped
- 1 teaspoon cumin, ground
- 1 teaspoon oregano

For serving:

- Chopped cilantro
- Chopped red onion
- Shredded cheddar cheese

Directions:

In your instant pot, mix chicken with enchilada sauce, stock, tomatoes, green chilies, salt, pepper, garlic, onion, cumin and oregano, stir, cover and cook on Manual for 15 minutes. Ladle soup into bowls, serve with chopped cilantro, red onion, and shredded cheese sprinkled all over. Enjoy!

Nutrition: calories 312, fat 7, fiber 2, carbs 8, protein 14

Okra and Beef Stew

Preparation time: 10 minutes
Cooking time: 30 minutes
Servings: 4

Ingredients:

- 1 yellow onion, chopped
- 1 pound beef, cubed
- 1 garlic clove, minced
- 2 cups chicken stock
- 1 cardamom pod
- 14 ounces okra
- 12 ounces tomato sauce
- Salt and black pepper to the taste
- 5 tablespoons parsley, chopped
- A drizzle of olive oil
- Juice of ½ lemon

For the marinade:

- ½ teaspoon onion powder
- ½ teaspoon garlic powder
- A pinch of salt
- 1 tablespoon 7- spice mix

Directions:

In a bowl, mix meat with 7-spice, a pinch of salt, onion and garlic powder, toss to coat and leave aside. Set your instant pot on Sauté mode, add a drizzle of olive oil, heat it up, add onion, garlic and cardamom, stir and cook for 3 minutes. Add meat, stir, brown for 2 minutes and mix with okra, stock, tomato sauce, salt and pepper, stir, cover and cook on Low for 20 minutes. Add lemon juice and parsley, stir, divide into bowls and serve. Enjoy!

Nutrition: calories 273, fat 8, fiber 4, carbs 8, protein 17

Beef and Cabbage Stew

Preparation time: 10 minutes
Cooking time: 1 hour and 20 minutes
Servings: 6

Ingredients:
- 2 and ½ pounds beef brisket
- 2 bay leaves
- 4 cups water
- 4 carrots, chopped
- 3 garlic cloves, chopped
- 1 cabbage head, roughly shredded
- Salt and black pepper to the taste
- 3 turnips, cut into quarters
- Horseradish sauce for serving

Directions:

Put the beef brisket in your instant pot, add water, salt, pepper, garlic and bay leaves, cover and cook at High for 1 hour. Add carrots, cabbage and turnips, stir, cover the pot again and cook on High for 6 minutes. Divide stew among plates and serve with horseradish sauce on top. Enjoy!

Nutrition: calories 293, fat 8, fiber 3, carbs 10, protein 17

Lamb Shanks and Carrots

Preparation time: 10 minutes
Cooking time: 35 minutes
Servings: 4

Ingredients:
- 4 lamb shanks
- 2 tablespoons olive oil
- 2 tablespoons coconut flour
- 1 yellow onion, chopped
- 3 carrots, sliced
- 2 garlic cloves, minced
- 2 tablespoons tomato paste
- 1 teaspoon oregano, dried
- 1 tomato, chopped
- 2 tablespoons water
- 4 ounces beef stock
- Salt and black pepper to the taste

Directions:

In a bowl, mix lamb shanks with flour, salt and pepper and toss. Set your instant pot on Sauté mode, add oil, heat it up, add lamb, brown for a couple of minutes on each side and transfer to a bowl. Add onion, oregano, carrots and garlic to the pot, stir and sauté for 5 minutes. Add tomato, tomato paste, water, stock and return lamb to pot as well. Stir, cover, cook on High for 25 minutes, divide everything between plates and serve. Enjoy!

Nutrition: calories 400, fat 14, fiber 3, carbs 7, protein 30

Pork with Lemon Sauce

Preparation time: 10 minutes
Cooking time: 1 hour
Servings: 4

Ingredients:
- 1 and ½ pounds pork shoulder, chopped
- 3 garlic cloves, minced
- 1 cinnamon stick
- 2 cloves
- 1 yellow onion, chopped
- Juice of 1 lemon
- Salt and black pepper to the taste
- 1 tablespoon ginger, grated
- ½ cup water
- 1 teaspoon rosemary, dried
- 2 tablespoons stevia
- 2 tablespoons coconut aminos
- 1 tablespoon olive oil

Directions:

Set your instant pot on Sauté mode, add oil, heat it up, add pork, salt and pepper, stir, brown for 5 minutes on each side and transfer to a plate. Add onions, ginger, garlic, lemon juice, water, stevia, aminos, rosemary, cinnamon, cloves, pork, salt and pepper to the pot, stir, heat up, cover pot and cook on Manual for 50 minutes. Discard cloves and cinnamon, stir pork mix, divide everything between plates and serve. Enjoy!

Nutrition: calories 310, fat 4, fiber 2, carbs 12, protein 24

Meatballs and Sauce

Preparation time: 10 minutes
Cooking time: 15 minutes
Servings: 8

Ingredients:
- 1 and ½ pounds pork meat, ground
- 1 egg
- 2 tablespoons parsley, chopped
- 4 tablespoons coconut flour
- 2 garlic cloves, minced
- Salt and black pepper to the taste
- ¾ cup beef stock
- ½ teaspoon nutmeg, ground
- ½ teaspoon sweet paprika
- 2 tablespoons olive oil
- 2 carrots, chopped
- 1 celeriac, cubed
- 1 bay leaf

Directions:

In a bowl, mix ground meat with egg, salt, pepper, parsley, paprika, garlic, 1 tablespoon stock and nutmeg, stir well and dust them with the coconut flour. Set your instant pot on Sauté mode, add oil, heat it up, add meatballs and brown them on all sides. Add carrots, bay leaf, celeriac and stock, stir, cover the pot and cook on High for 8 minutes. Discard bay leaf, divide meatballs and sauce into bowls and serve. Enjoy!

Nutrition: calories 383, fat 10, fiber 6, carbs 10, protein 15

Salmon and Veggies

Preparation time: 10 minutes
Cooking time: 15 minutes
Servings: 4

Ingredients:

- 4 salmon fillets, boneless
- 2 cups water
- 3 tablespoons olive oil
- 1 lemon, sliced
- 1 white onion, chopped
- 3 tomatoes, sliced
- 4 thyme sprigs, chopped
- 4 parsley sprigs, chopped
- Salt and black pepper to the taste

Directions:

Drizzle the oil on a parchment paper. Add a layer of tomatoes, salt and pepper. Drizzle some oil again, add fish and season with salt and pepper. Drizzle some more oil, add thyme and parsley, onions, lemon slices, salt and pepper and wrap packet. Add the water to your instant pot, add the steamer basket, add packet inside, cover and cook on High for 15 minutes. Unwrap packet, divide fish and veggies between plates and serve. Enjoy!

Nutrition: calories 200, fat 5, fiber 7, carbs 10, protein 20

Shrimp and Turnips

Preparation time: 10 minutes
Cooking time: 15 minutes
Servings: 4

Ingredients:

- 2 pounds shrimp, peeled and deveined
- 1 pound tomatoes, peeled and chopped
- 1 cup water
- 3 turnips, cut into quarters
- 4 tablespoons olive oil
- 4 onions, chopped
- 1 teaspoon coriander, ground
- 1 teaspoon curry powder
- Juice of 1 lemon
- A pinch of salt and black pepper

Directions:

Put the water in your instant pot, add steamer basket, add turnips, cover pot, cook on High for 6 minutes, drain, transfer to a bowl and leave aside for now. Clean your instant pot, set it on sauté mode, add oil, heat it up, add onions, stir and cook for 5 minutes. Add salt, coriander, curry, tomatoes, lemon juice, shrimp and turnips, stir, cover and cook on High for 6 minutes more. Divide shrimp into bowls and serve. Enjoy!

Nutrition: calories 183, fat 4, fiber 1, carbs 7, protein 15

Squid and Veggies

Preparation time: 10 minutes
Cooking time: 27 minutes
Servings: 4

Ingredients:

- 1 pound squid, cleaned and chopped
- 10 garlic cloves, minced
- 2-inch ginger piece, grated
- 2 green chilies, chopped
- ½ tablespoon lemon juice
- 2 yellow onions, chopped
- 1 curry leaf
- 1 tablespoon coriander powder
- ¼ cup coconut, shredded
- ¾ tablespoon chili powder
- 1 teaspoon garam masala
- Salt and black pepper to the taste
- A pinch of turmeric
- 1 teaspoon mustard seeds
- ¾ cup water
- 3 tablespoons olive oil

Directions:

Set your instant pot on Sauté mode, add oil, heat it up, add mustard seeds and coconut, stir and cook for 2 minutes. Add ginger, onions, garlic, chilies, salt, pepper, curry leaf, coriander powder, chili powder, garam masala, turmeric, water, lemon juice and squid, stir, cover and cook on Low for 25 minutes. Divide into bowls and serve right away. Enjoy!

Nutrition: calories 193, fat 7, fiber 1, carbs 7, protein 19

Artichokes and Sauce

Preparation time: 10 minutes
Cooking time: 20 minutes
Servings: 4

Ingredients:

- 4 artichokes, trimmed
- 2 cups chicken stock
- 1 tablespoon tarragon, chopped
- 4 lemon slices
- Zest from 1 lemon, grated
- Pulp from 1 lemon
- 1 celery stalk, chopped
- ½ cup olive oil
- Salt to the taste

Directions:

Put artichokes in your instant pot, add lemon slices on top, add stock, cover, cook on High for 20 minutes and transfer them to a platter. Meanwhile, in your food processor, mix tarragon with lemon zest, lemon pulp, celery, salt and olive oil, pulse very well, drizzle this over artichokes and serve right away. Enjoy!

Nutrition: calories 192, fat 6, fiber 7, carbs 9, protein 7

Squash and Chicken Cream

Preparation time: 10 minutes
Cooking time: 16 minutes
Servings: 6

Ingredients:

- 1 and ½ pounds butternut squash, baked, peeled and cubed
- 1 cup chicken meat, cooked and shredded
- ½ cup green onions, chopped
- 3 tablespoons ghee
- 30 ounces chicken stock
- ½ cup carrots, chopped
- ½ cup celery, chopped
- 1 garlic clove, minced
- ½ teaspoon Italian seasoning
- 15 ounces canned tomatoes and their juice, chopped
- Salt and black pepper to the taste
- A pinch of red pepper flakes, dried
- A pinch of nutmeg, grated
- 1 and ½ cup coconut cream

Directions:

Set your instant pot on Sauté mode, add ghee, melt it, add celery, carrots and onions, stir and cook for 3 minutes. Add garlic, squash, tomatoes, stock, Italian seasoning, salt, pepper, pepper flakes and nutmeg, stir, cover and cook on High for 10 minutes. Blend soup using an immersion blender, add coconut cream and chicken, stir, set the pot on simmer mode and cook for 3 minutes more. Ladle into bowls and serve. Enjoy!

Nutrition: calories 182, fat 2, fiber 7, carbs 10, protein 7

Veggie Soup

Preparation time: 10 minutes
Cooking time: 12 minutes
Servings: 8

Ingredients:

- 1 tablespoon olive oil
- 1 celery stalk, chopped
- 3 pounds tomatoes, chopped
- 2 carrots, chopped
- 1 onion, chopped
- 1 zucchini, chopped
- 4 garlic cloves, minced
- 30 ounces canned chicken stock
- Salt and black pepper to the taste
- 1 teaspoon Italian seasoning
- 2 cups baby spinach
- 1 cup asiago cheese, grated
- 2 tablespoons basil, chopped

Directions:

Set your instant pot on Sauté mode, add oil, heat it up, add onion, stir and cook for 5 minutes. Add carrots, garlic, celery, zucchini, tomatoes, stock, Italian seasoning, salt and pepper, stir, cover and cook on High for 6 minutes. Add basil and spinach, stir, ladle into bowls and serve with cheese sprinkled on top. Enjoy!

Nutrition: calories 172, fat 4, fiber 4, carbs 10, protein 6

Cabbage and Carrot Soup

Preparation time: 10 minutes
Cooking time: 10 minutes
Servings: 4

Ingredients:
- 1 cabbage head, shredded
- 1 small yellow onion, chopped
- 12 ounces baby carrots
- 3 celery stalks, chopped
- 2 tablespoons olive oil
- 3 teaspoons garlic, minced
- ¼ cup cilantro, chopped
- 4 cups chicken stock
- Salt and black pepper to the taste

Directions:

In your instant pot, mix cabbage with celery, carrots, onion, stock, olive oil and garlic, stir, cover and cook on High for 8 minutes. Add salt, pepper and cilantro, stir well, ladle into soup bowls and serve. Enjoy!

Nutrition: calories 165, fat 4, fiber 3, carbs 9, protein 10

Asparagus Cream

Preparation time: 10 minutes
Cooking time: 25 minutes
Servings: 4

Ingredients:
- 2 pounds green asparagus, trimmed and cut into medium pieces
- 3 tablespoons ghee
- 6 cups chicken stock
- 1 yellow onion, chopped
-
- ¼ teaspoon lemon juice
- ½ cup coconut cream
- Salt and white pepper to the taste

Directions:

Set your instant pot on Sauté mode, add ghee, heat it up, add asparagus, onion, salt and pepper, stir and cook for 5 minutes. Add stock, cover pot, cook on Low for 15 minutes, transfer everything to your blender and pulse well. Return soup to pot, add coconut cream and lemon juice, stir, ladle into bowls and serve. Enjoy!

Nutrition: calories 100, fat 5, fiber 1, carbs 8, protein 7

Fresh Fennel and Leek Soup

Preparation time: 10 minutes
Cooking time: 15 minutes
Servings: 2

Ingredients:

- 1 fennel bulb, chopped
- 2 cups water
- 1 bay leaf
- 1 leek, chopped

- 1 tablespoon olive oil
- Salt and black pepper to the taste
- 2 teaspoons parmesan cheese, grated

Directions:

In your instant pot, mix fennel with leek, bay leaf, oil, water, salt and pepper, stir, cover and cook on High for 15 minutes. Add cheese, stir, ladle into bowls and serve. Enjoy!

Nutrition: calories 126, fat 3, fiber 3, carbs 6, protein 5

Chicken Stew

Preparation time: 10 minutes
Cooking time: 40 minutes
Servings: 6

Ingredients:

- 6 chicken thighs
- 1 teaspoon olive oil
- ¼ pound baby carrots
- Salt and black pepper to the taste
- 1 yellow onion, chopped

- 2 tablespoons tomato paste
- 1 celery stalk, chopped
- ½ teaspoon thyme, dried
- 2 and ½ cups chicken stock
- 15 ounces canned tomatoes, chopped

Directions:

Set your instant pot on Sauté mode, add oil, heat it up, add chicken, salt and pepper, brown for 4 minutes on each side and transfer to a plate. Add celery, onion, tomato paste, carrots, thyme, salt and pepper, stir and sauté them for 4 minutes more. Add stock, chicken and tomatoes; cover and cook on High for 25 minutes. Transfer chicken pieces to a cutting board, leave aside to cool down for a few minutes, discard bones, shred meat and return it to the stew. Stir, divide into bowls and serve hot. Enjoy!

Nutrition: calories 182, fat 4, fiber 4, carbs 7, protein 14

Turkey Stew

Preparation time: 10 minutes
Cooking time: 33 minutes
Servings: 4

Ingredients:

- 1 tablespoon avocado oil
- 1 yellow onion, chopped
- 1 teaspoon garlic, minced
- 3 celery stalks, chopped
- 2 carrots, chopped
- Salt and black pepper to the taste
- 3 cups turkey meat, already cooked and shredded
- 15 ounces canned tomatoes, chopped
- 5 cups turkey stock
- 1 tablespoon cranberry sauce

Directions:

Set your instant pot on Sauté mode, add oil, heat it up, add carrots, celery and onions, stir and cook for 3 minutes. Add tomatoes, stock, garlic, meat, cranberry sauce, salt and pepper, stir, cover, cook on Low for 30 minutes, divide into bowls and serve. Enjoy!

Nutrition: calories 200, fat 4, fiber 1, carbs 6, protein 16

Mushroom Stew

Preparation time: 10 minutes
Cooking time: 20 minutes
Servings: 6

Ingredients:

- 1 tablespoon olive oil
- 1 celery stalk, chopped
- 1 and ½ cups beef stock
- 1 red onion, chopped
- 2 pounds beef chuck, cubed
- 1 teaspoon rosemary, chopped
- Salt and black pepper to the taste
- 1 ounce porcini mushrooms, chopped
- 2 carrots, chopped
- 2 tablespoons coconut flour
- 2 tablespoons ghee

Directions:

Set your instant pot on Sauté mode, add oil, heat it up, add beef, stir and brown for 5 minutes. Add onion, celery, rosemary, salt, pepper, carrots, mushrooms and stock, stir, cover and cook on High for 15 minutes. Heat up a pan with the ghee over medium high heat, melt it, add flour and 3 tablespoons cooking juices from the stew, stir, add to stew, set the pot on simmer mode and cook everything for 4 minutes more. Divide into bowls and serve. Enjoy!

Nutrition: calories 283, fat 4, fiber 3, carbs 8, protein 18

Stuffed Bell Peppers

Preparation time: 10 minutes
Cooking time: 12 minutes
Servings: 4

Ingredients:

- 4 bell peppers, tops and seeds removed and blanched in hot water for 3 minutes
- Salt and black pepper to the taste
- 16 ounces beef meat, ground
- 1 egg
- ½ cup coconut milk
- 2 onions, chopped
- 8 ounces water
- 10 ounces keto tomato soup

Directions:

In a bowl, mix beef with salt, pepper, egg, milk and onions and stir very well. Stuff bell peppers with this mix, place them in your instant pot, add tomato soup and water, cover and cook on High for 12 minutes. Divide stuffed peppers between plates, drizzle cooking juices all over and serve. Enjoy!

Nutrition: calories 182, fat 2, fiber 3, carbs 7, protein 10

Crab Legs

Preparation time: 5 minutes
Cooking time: 3 minutes
Servings: 4

Ingredients:

- 4 pounds crab legs, halved
- 3 lemon wedges
- ¼ cup ghee
- 1 cup water

Directions:

Put the water in your instant pot, add steamer basket, add crab legs inside, cover and cook on High for 3 minutes. Transfer crab legs to a bowl, add melted ghee, toss and serve them with lemon wedges on the side. Enjoy!

Nutrition: calories 100, fat 4, fiber 1, carbs 2, protein 7

Ketogenic Instant Pot Snacks and Appetizer Recipes

Cranberry Dip

Preparation time: 10 minutes
Cooking time: 4 minutes
Servings: 4

Ingredients:

- 2 and ½ teaspoons lemon zest, grated
- 3 tablespoons lemon juice
- 12 ounces cranberries
- 4 tablespoons stevia

Directions:

In your instant pot, mix lemon juice with stevia, lemon zest and cranberries, stir, cover and cook on High for 2 minutes. Set the pot on simmer mode, stir your dip for a couple more minutes, transfer to a bowl and serve with some biscuits as a snack. Enjoy!

Nutrition: calories 73, fat 0, fiber 1, carbs 2, protein 2

Chili Dip

Preparation time: 10 minutes
Cooking time: 10 minutes
Servings: 8

Ingredients:

- 5 ancho chilies, dried and chopped
- 2 garlic cloves, minced
- Slat and black pepper to the taste
- 1 and ½ cups water
- 2 tablespoons balsamic vinegar
- 1 and ½ teaspoons stevia
- 1 tablespoon oregano, chopped
- ½ teaspoon cumin, ground

Directions:

In your instant pot mix water chilies, garlic, salt, pepper, stevia, cumin and oregano, stir, cover and cook on High for 8 minutes. Blend using an immersion blender, add vinegar, stir, set the pot on simmer mode and cook your chili dip until it thickens. Serve with veggie sticks on the side as a snack. Enjoy!

Nutrition: calories 85, fat 1, fiber 1, carbs 2, protein 2

Zucchini Dip

Preparation time: 10 minutes
Cooking time: 10 minutes
Servings: 4

Ingredients:

- 1 yellow onion, chopped
- 1 and ½ pounds zucchini, chopped
- 1 tablespoon olive oil
- 2 garlic cloves, minced
- Salt and white pepper to the taste
- ½ cup water
- 1 bunch basil, chopped

Directions:

Set your instant pot on Sauté mode, add oil, heat it up, add onion, stir and sauté for 3 minutes. Add zucchini, salt, pepper and water, stir, cover and cook on High for 3 minutes. Add garlic and basil, blend everything using an immersion blender, set the pot on simmer mode and cook your dip for a few more minutes until it thickens. Transfer to a bowl and serve as a tasty snack. Enjoy!

Nutrition: calories 100, fat 2, fiber 3, carbs 4, protein 2

Beets and Squash Dip

Preparation time: 10 minutes
Cooking time: 20 minutes
Servings: 8

Ingredients:

- 1 yellow onion, chopped
- 2 tablespoons olive oil
- 5 celery ribs
- 8 garlic cloves, minced
- 8 carrots, chopped
- 4 beets, peeled and chopped
- 1 butternut squash, peeled and chopped
- 1 cup veggie stock
- ¼ cup lemon juice
- 1 bunch basil, chopped
- 2 bay leaves
- Salt and black pepper to the taste

Directions:

Set your instant pot on Sauté mode, add oil, heat it up, add celery, carrots and onions, stir and cook for 3 minutes. Add beets, squash, garlic, stock, lemon juice, basil, bay leaves, salt and pepper, stir, cover and cook on High for 12 minutes. Discard bay leaves, blend dip using an immersion blender, transfer to a bowl and serve as a snack. Enjoy!

Nutrition: calories 83, fat 1, fiber 3, carbs 4, protein 3

Cheese and Sausage Dip

Preparation time: 10 minutes
Cooking time: 5 minutes
Servings: 4

Ingredients:

- 2 cups Mexican cheese, cut into chunks
- 1 cup Italian sausage, cooked and chopped
- 5 ounces canned tomatoes and green chilies, chopped
- 4 tablespoons water

Directions:

In your instant pot, mix sausage with cheese, tomatoes and chilies and water, stir, cover, cook on High for 5 minutes, blend a bit using an immersion blender, transfer to a bowl and serve as a dip. Enjoy!

Nutrition: calories 100, fat 3, fiber 2, carbs 6, protein 4

Creamy Mushroom Dip

Preparation time: 10 minutes
Cooking time: 35 minutes
Servings: 6

Ingredients:

- 1 yellow onion, chopped
- ¼ cup olive oil
- 1 tablespoon coconut flour
- 1 tablespoons thyme, chopped
- Salt and black pepper to the taste
- 3 garlic cloves, minced
- 1 and ¼ cup chicken stock
- 10 ounces shiitake mushrooms, chopped
- 10 ounces cremini mushrooms, chopped
- 10 ounces Portobello mushrooms, chopped
- 1 ounce parmesan cheese, grated
- ½ cup coconut cream
- 1 tablespoons parsley, chopped

Directions:

Set your instant pot on Sauté mode, add oil, heat it up, add onion, salt, pepper, flour, garlic and thyme, stir well and cook for 5 minutes. Add stock, shiitake, cremini and Portobello mushrooms, stir, cover and cook on High for 25 minutes. Add cream, cheese and parsley, stir, set the pot on Simmer mode, cook dip for 5 minutes more, transfer to bowls and serve as a dip. Enjoy!

Nutrition: calories 152, fat 5, fiber 4, carbs 10, protein 6

Cauliflower Dip

Preparation time: 10 minutes
Cooking time: 10 minutes
Servings: 6

Ingredients:
- 2 tablespoons ghee
- 8 garlic cloves, minced
- 7 cups veggie stock
- 6 cups cauliflower florets
- Salt and black pepper to the taste
- ½ cup coconut milk

Directions:
Set your instant pot on Sauté mode, add ghee, heat it up, add garlic, salt and pepper, stir and cook for 2 minutes. Add stock and cauliflower to the pot, heat up, cover and cook on High for 7 minutes. Transfer cauliflower and 1 cup stock to your blender, add milk and blend well for a few minutes. Transfer to a bowl and serve as a dip for veggies. Enjoy!

Nutrition: calories 100, fat 4, fiber 4, carbs 7, protein 7

Spicy Mango Dip

Preparation time: 10 minutes
Cooking time: 13 minutes
Servings: 4

Ingredients:
- 1 shallot, chopped
- 1 tablespoon coconut oil
- ¼ teaspoon cardamom powder
- 2 tablespoons ginger, minced
- ½ teaspoon cinnamon powder
- 2 mangos, peeled and chopped
- 2 red hot chilies, chopped
- 1 apple, cored and chopped
- ¼ cup raisins
- 5 tablespoons stevia
- 1 and ¼ apple cider vinegar

Directions:
Set your instant pot on Sauté mode, add oil, heat it up, add shallot and ginger, stir and cook for 3 minutes. Add cinnamon, hot peppers, cardamom, mangos, apple, raisins, stevia and cider, stir, cover and cook on High for 7 minutes. Set the pot on simmer mode, cook your dip for 6 minutes more, transfer to bowls and serve cold as a snack. Enjoy!

Nutrition: calories 100, fat 2, fiber 1, carbs 3, protein 1

Tomato Dip

Preparation time: 10 minutes
Cooking time: 15 minutes
Servings: 20

Ingredients:

- 2 pounds tomatoes, peeled and chopped
- 1 apple, cored and chopped
- 1 yellow onion, chopped
- 3 ounces dates chopped
- Salt to the taste
- 3 teaspoons whole spice
- ½ pint balsamic vinegar
- 4 tablespoons stevia

Directions:

Put tomatoes, apple, onion, dates, salt, whole spice and half of the vinegar in your instant pot, stir, cover and cook on High for 10 minutes. Set the pot on simmer mode, add the rest of the vinegar and stevia, stir, cook for a few minutes more until it thickens, transfer to bowls and serve as a snack. Enjoy!

Nutrition: calories 100, fat 3, fiber 3, carbs 6, protein 2

Mustard and Mushrooms Dip

Preparation time: 10 minutes
Cooking time: 10 minutes
Servings: 4

Ingredients:

- 6 ounces mushrooms, chopped
- 3 tablespoon olive oil
- 1 thyme sprigs
- 1 garlic clove, minced
- 4 ounces beef stock
- 1 tablespoon balsamic vinegar
- 1 tablespoon mustard
- 2 tablespoon coconut cream
- 2 tablespoons parsley, finely chopped

Directions:

Set your instant pot on Sauté mode, add oil, heat it up, add thyme, mushrooms and garlic, stir and sauté for 4 minutes. Add vinegar and stock, stir, cover, cook on High for 3 minutes, discard thyme, add mustard, coconut cream and parsley, stir, set the pot on simmer mode and cook for 3 minutes more. Divide into bowls and serve as a snack. Enjoy!

Nutrition: calories 100, fat 3, fiber 2, carbs 4, protein 3

Artichoke Dip

Preparation time: 10 minutes
Cooking time: 5 minutes
Servings: 6

Ingredients:
- 14 ounces canned artichoke hearts
- 8 ounces cream cheese
- 8 ounces mozzarella cheese, shredded
- 16 ounces parmesan cheese, grated
- 10 ounces spinach, torn
- 1 teaspoon onion powder
- ½ cup chicken stock
- ½ cup coconut cream
- 3 garlic cloves, minced
- ½ cup mayonnaise

Directions:
In your instant pot, mix artichokes with stock, garlic, spinach, cream cheese, coconut cream, onion powder and mayo, stir, cover and cook on High for 5 minutes. Add mozzarella and parmesan, stir well, transfer to a bowl and serve as a snack. Enjoy!

Nutrition: calories 200, fat 3, fiber 0, carbs 4, protein 7

Asparagus and Prosciutto Appetizer

Preparation time: 5 minutes
Cooking time: 4 minutes
Servings: 4

Ingredients:
- 8 asparagus spears
- 8 ounces prosciutto slices
- 2 cups water
- A pinch of salt

Directions:
Wrap asparagus spears in prosciutto slices and place them on a cutting board. Add the water to your instant pot, add a pinch of salt, add steamer basket, place asparagus inside, cover and cook on High for 4 minutes. Arrange asparagus on a platter and serve as an appetizer. Enjoy!

Nutrition: calories 83, fat 3, fiber 2, carbs 6, protein 3

Salmon Patties

Preparation time: 10 minutes
Cooking time: 7 minutes
Servings: 4

Ingredients:

- 1 teaspoon olive oil
- 1 egg, whisked
- 4 tablespoons coconut flour
- 1 pound salmon meat, minced
- 2 tablespoons lemon zest, grated
- Salt and black pepper to the taste
- Arugula leaves for serving

Directions:

Put salmon in your food processor, blend it, transfer to a bowl, add salt, pepper, lemon zest, coconut and egg, stir well and shape small patties out of this mix. Set your instant pot on sauté mode, add oil, heat it up, add patties and cook them for 3 minutes on each side. Arrange arugula on a platter, add salmon patties on top and serve as an appetizer. Enjoy!

Nutrition: calories 162, fat 3, fiber 2, carbs 6, protein 16

Cod Puddings

Preparation time: 10 minutes
Cooking time: 20 minutes
Servings: 4

Ingredients:

- 1 pound cod fillets, skinless, boneless cut into medium pieces
- 2 tablespoons parsley, chopped
- 4 ounces coconut flour
- 2 teaspoons lemon juice
- 2 eggs, whisked
- 2 ounces ghee, melted
- ½ pint coconut milk, hot
- ½ pint shrimp sauce
- Salt and black pepper to the taste
- ½ pint water

Directions:

In a bowl, mix fish with flour, lemon juice, shrimp sauce, parsley, eggs, salt and pepper and stir. Add milk and melted ghee, stir well and leave aside for a couple of minutes. Divide this mix greased ramekins. Add the water to your instant pot, add the steamer basket, add puddings inside, cover and cook on High for 15 minutes. Serve the warm. Enjoy!

Nutrition: calories 172, fat 3, fiber 2, carbs 5, protein 6

Mussels Appetizer

Preparation time: 10 minutes
Cooking time: 7 minutes
Servings: 4

Ingredients:
- 2 pounds mussels, cleaned and scrubbed
- 1 white onion, chopped
- ½ cup veggie stock
- 2 garlic cloves, minced
- ½ cup water
- A drizzle of extra virgin olive oil

Directions:
Set instant pot on Sauté mode, add oil, heat it up, garlic and onion, stir and cook for 4 minutes. Add stock, stir and cook for 1 minute. Add the steamer basket, add mussels inside, cover and cook on High for 2 minutes. Arrange mussels on a platter and serve with some of the cooking juices drizzled all over. Enjoy!

Nutrition: calories 82, fat 3, fiber 2, carbs 3, protein 2

Italian Mussels Appetizer

Preparation time: 10 minutes
Cooking time: 10 minutes
Servings: 4

Ingredients:
- 28 ounces canned tomatoes, chopped
- 2 pounds mussels, scrubbed
- 2 jalapeno peppers, chopped
- ½ cup white onion, chopped
- ¼ cup veggie stock
- ¼ cup olive oil
- ¼ cup balsamic vinegar
- 2 tablespoons red pepper flakes, crushed
- 2 garlic cloves, minced
- Salt to the taste
- ½ cup basil, chopped

Directions:
Set your instant pot on Sauté mode, add oil heat it up, add tomatoes, onion, jalapenos, stock, vinegar, garlic and pepper flakes, stir and cook for 5 minutes. Add mussels, stir, cover, cook on Low for 4 minutes, add salt and basil, stir, divide everything into small bowls and serve as an appetizer. Enjoy!

Nutrition: calories 82, fat 1, fiber 2, carbs 2, protein 6

Spicy Mussels

Preparation time: 10 minutes
Cooking time: 6 minutes
Servings: 4

Ingredients:

- 2 pounds mussels, scrubbed
- 2 tablespoons olive oil
- 1 yellow onion, chopped
- ½ cup chicken stock
- ½ teaspoon red pepper flakes
- 14 ounces tomatoes, chopped
- 2 teaspoons garlic, minced
- 2 teaspoons oregano, dried

Directions:

Set your instant pot on Sauté mode, add oil, heat it up, add onions, stir and sauté for 3 minutes. Add pepper flakes, garlic, stock, tomatoes, oregano and mussels, stir, cover and cook on Low for 3 minutes. Divide mussels into small bowls and serve as an appetizer. Enjoy!

Nutrition: calories 82, fat 1, fiber 2, carbs 3, protein 2

Mussels Bowls

Preparation time: 5 minutes
Cooking time: 7 minutes
Servings: 4

Ingredients:

- 2 pounds mussels, scrubbed
- 12 ounces veggie stock
- 1 tablespoon olive oil
- 1 yellow onion, chopped
- 8 ounces spicy sausage, chopped
- 1 tablespoon sweet paprika

Directions:

Set your instant pot on Sauté mode, add oil, heat it up, add onion and sausages, stir and cook for 5 minutes. Add stock, paprika and mussels, stir, cover, cook on Low for 2 minutes, divide into bowls and serve as an appetizer. Enjoy!

Nutrition: calories 112, fat 4, fiber 2, carbs 4, protein 10

Clams and Mussels

Preparation time: 10 minutes
Cooking time: 13 minutes
Servings: 4

Ingredients:

- 15 small clams
- 30 mussels, scrubbed
- 2 chorizo links, sliced
- 1 yellow onion, chopped
- 10 ounces veggie stock
- 2 tablespoons parsley, chopped
- 1 teaspoon olive oil
- Lemon wedges for serving

Directions:

Set your instant pot on Sauté mode, add oil, heat it up, add onion and chorizo, stir and cook for 3 minutes. Add clams, mussels and stock, stir, cover, cook on High for 10 minutes, add parsley, stir, divide into bowls and serve as an appetizer with lemon wedges on the side. Enjoy!

Nutrition: calories 172, fat 4, fiber 3, carbs 7, protein 12

Stuffed Clams

Preparation time: 10 minutes
Cooking time: 4 minutes
Servings: 4

Ingredients:

- 24 clams, shucked
- 3 garlic cloves, minced
- 4 tablespoons ghee
- ¼ cup parsley, chopped
- ¼ cup parmesan cheese, grated
- 1 teaspoon oregano, dried
- 1 cup almonds, crushed
- 2 cups water
- Lemon wedges

Directions:

In a bowl, mix crushed almonds with parmesan, oregano, parsley, butter and garlic, stir and divide this into exposed clams. Add the water to your instant pot, add steamer basket, add clams inside, cover and cook on High for 4 minutes. Arrange clams on a platter and serve them as an appetizer with lemon wedges on the side. Enjoy!

Nutrition: calories 92, fat 3, fiber 3, carbs 6, protein 5

Shrimp and Sausage Appetizer Bowls

Preparation time: 10 minutes
Cooking time: 5 minutes
Servings: 4

Ingredients:

- 1 and ½ pounds shrimp, heads removed
- 12 ounces sausage, cooked and chopped
- 1 tablespoon old bay seasoning
- 16 ounces chicken stock
- Salt and black pepper to the taste
- 1 teaspoon red pepper flakes, crushed
- 2 sweet onions, cut into wedges
- 8 garlic cloves, minced

Directions:

In your instant pot, mix stock with old bay seasoning, pepper flakes, salt, black pepper, onions, garlic, sausage and shrimp, stir, cover and cook on High for 5 minutes. Divide into small bowls and serve as an appetizer. Enjoy!

Nutrition: calories 251, fat 4, fiber 3, carbs 6, protein 7

Asian Shrimp Appetizer

Preparation time: 10 minutes
Cooking time: 4 minutes
Servings: 4

Ingredients:

- 1 pounds shrimp, peeled and deveined
- 2 tablespoons coconut aminos
- 3 tablespoons vinegar
- ¾ cup pineapple juice
- 1 cup chicken stock
- 3 tablespoons stevia

Directions:

Put shrimp, pineapple juice, stock, aminos and stevia in your instant pot, stir a bit, cover and cook on High for 4 minutes. Arrange shrimp on a platter, drizzle cooking juices all over and serve as an appetizer. Enjoy!

Nutrition: calories 172, fat 4, fiber 1, carbs 3, protein 20

Mediterranean Octopus Appetizer

Preparation time: 10 minutes
Cooking time: 16 minutes
Servings: 6

Ingredients:

- 1 octopus, cleaned and prepared
- 2 rosemary sprigs
- 2 teaspoons oregano, dried
- ½ yellow onion, chopped

For the marinade:

- ¼ cup extra virgin olive oil
- Juice of ½ lemon
- 4 garlic cloves, minced

- 4 thyme sprigs
- ½ lemon
- 1 teaspoon black peppercorns
- 3 tablespoons olive oil

- 2 thyme sprigs
- 1 rosemary sprigs
- Salt and black pepper to the taste

Directions:

Put the octopus in your instant pot, add oregano, 2 rosemary sprigs, 4 thyme sprigs, onion, lemon, 3 tablespoons olive oil, peppercorns and salt, stir, cover, cook on High for 10 minutes, transfer to a cutting board, cool it down, separate tentacles and transfer them to a bowl. Add ¼ cup olive oil, lemon juice, garlic, 1 rosemary sprigs, 2 thyme sprigs, salt and pepper, toss to coat and leave aside for 1 hour. Place octopus on preheated grill over medium high heat, cook for 3 minutes on each side, arrange on a platter and serve. Enjoy!

Nutrition: calories 162, fat 3, fiber 1, carbs 2, protein 7

Chinese Squid Appetizer

Preparation time: 10 minutes
Cooking time: 15 minutes
Servings: 4

Ingredients:

- 4 squid, tentacles from 1 squid separated and chopped
- 1 cup cauliflower rice
- 14 ounces fish stock

- 4 tablespoons coconut aminos
- 1 tablespoon mirin
- 2 tablespoons stevia

Directions:

In a bowl, mix chopped tentacles with cauliflower rice, stir well and stuff each squid with the mix. Place squid in your instant pot, add stock, aminos, mirin and stevia, stir, cover and cook on High for 15 minutes. Arrange stuffed squid on a platter and serve as an appetizer. Enjoy!

Nutrition: calories 162, fat 2, fiber 2, carbs 3, protein 10

Simple Artichokes

Preparation time: 10 minutes
Cooking time: 15 minutes
Servings: 4

Ingredients:

- 4 big artichokes, trimmed
- Salt and black pepper to the taste
- 2 tablespoons lemon juice
- ¼ cup olive oil
- 2 teaspoons balsamic vinegar
- 1 teaspoon oregano, dried
- 2 garlic cloves, minced
- 2 cups water

Directions:

Add the water to your instant pot, add the steamer basket, add artichokes inside, cover and cook on High for 8 minutes. In a bowl, mix lemon juice with vinegar, oil, salt, pepper, garlic and oregano and stir very well. Cut artichokes in halves, add them to lemon and vinegar mix, toss well, place them on preheated grill over medium high heat, cook for 3 minutes on each side, arrange them on a platter and serve as an appetizer. Enjoy!

Nutrition: calories 162, fat 4, fiber 2, carbs 3, protein 5

Cajun Shrimp

Preparation time: 4 minutes
Cooking time: 3 minutes
Servings: 4

Ingredients:

- 1 cup water
- 1 pound shrimp, peeled and deveined
- ½ tablespoon Cajun seasoning
- 1 teaspoon extra virgin olive oil
- 1 bunch asparagus, trimmed

Directions:

Put the water in your instant pot, add steamer basket, add shrimp and asparagus inside, drizzle Cajun seasoning and oil over them, toss a bit, cover pot and cook on High for 3 minutes. Arrange on appetizer plates and serve as an appetizer. Enjoy!

Nutrition: calories 152, fat 2, fiber 3, carbs 8, protein 15

French Endives

Preparation time: 10 minutes
Cooking time: 7 minutes
Servings: 4

Ingredients:

- 4 endives, trimmed and halved
- Salt and black pepper to the taste
- 1 tablespoon lemon juice
- 1 tablespoon ghee

Directions:

Set your instant pot on Sauté mode, add ghee, heat it up, add endives, season with salt and pepper, drizzle lemon juice, cover pot and cook them on High for 7 minutes. Arrange endives on a platter, drizzle some of the cooking juice over them and serve as an appetizer. Enjoy!

Nutrition: calories 100, fat 3, fiber 2, carbs 7, protein 2

Endives and Ham Appetizer

Preparation time: 10 minutes
Cooking time: 20 minutes
Servings: 4

Ingredients:

- 4 endives, trimmed
- 1 cup water
- Salt and black pepper to the taste
- 1 tablespoon coconut flour
- 2 tablespoons ghee
- 4 slices ham
- ½ teaspoon nutmeg, ground
- 14 ounces coconut milk

Directions:

Add the water to your instant pot, add steamer basket, add endives inside, cover, cook them on High for 10 minutes, wrap them in ham and transfer them to a baking dish. Clean your instant pot, set it on simmer mode, add the ghee, heat it up, add coconut flour, milk, salt, pepper and nutmeg, stir and cook for 7 minutes. Pour milk and nutmeg mix over endives, introduce them in preheated broiler and broil for 10 minutes. Arrange on a platter and serve as an appetizer. Enjoy!

Nutrition: calories 152, fat 3, fiber 3, carbs 6, protein 12

Eggplant Spread

Preparation time: 10 minutes
Cooking time: 10 minutes
Servings: 6

Ingredients:

- 2 pounds eggplant, peeled and cut into medium chunks
- Salt and black pepper to the taste
- ¼ cup olive oil
- 4 garlic cloves, minced
- ½ cup water
- 3 olives, pitted and sliced
- ¼ cup lemon juice
- 1 bunch thyme, chopped
- 1 tablespoon sesame seed paste

Directions:

Set your instant pot on sauté mode, add oil, heat it up, add eggplant pieces, stir and cook for 5 minutes. Add garlic, water, salt and pepper, stir, cover, cook on High for 3 minutes, transfer to a blender, add sesame seed paste, lemon juice and thyme, stir and pulse really well. Transfer to bowls, sprinkle olive slices on top and serve as an appetizer. Enjoy!

Nutrition: calories 87, fat 4, fiber 2, carbs 6, protein 2

Okra Bowls

Preparation time: 10 minutes
Cooking time: 15 minutes
Servings: 6

Ingredients:

- 1 pound okra, trimmed
- 6 scallions, chopped
- 3 green bell peppers, chopped
- Salt and black pepper to the taste
- 2 tablespoons olive oil
- 1 teaspoon stevia
- 28 ounces canned tomatoes, chopped

Directions:

Set your instant pot on Sauté mode, add oil, heat it up, add scallions and bell peppers, stir and cook for 5 minutes. Add okra, salt, pepper, stevia and tomatoes, stir, cover, cook on High for 10 minutes, divide into small bowls and serve as an appetizer salad. Enjoy!

Nutrition: calories 121, fat 3, fiber 3, carbs 6, protein 4

Easy Leeks Platter

Preparation time: 10 minutes
Cooking time: 10 minutes
Servings: 4

Ingredients:
- 4 leeks, washed, roots and ends cut off
- Salt and black pepper to the taste
- 1/3 cup water
- 1 tablespoon ghee

Directions:
Put leeks in your instant pot, add water, ghee, salt and pepper, stir, cover and cook on High for 5 minutes. Set the pot on sauté mode, cook leeks for a couple more minutes, arrange them on a platter and serve as an appetizer. Enjoy!

Nutrition: calories 73, fat 3, fiber 4, carbs 9, protein 7

Tomatoes Appetizer

Preparation time: 10 minutes
Cooking time: 10 minutes
Servings: 4

Ingredients:
- 4 tomatoes, tops cut off and pulp scooped
- ½ cup water
- Salt and black pepper to the taste
- 1 yellow onion, chopped
- 1 tablespoon ghee
- 2 tablespoons celery, chopped
- ½ cup mushrooms, chopped
- 1 cup cottage cheese
- ¼ teaspoon caraway seeds
- 1 tablespoon parsley, chopped

Directions:
Set your instant pot on sauté mode, add ghee, heat it up, add onion and celery, stir and cook for 3 minutes. Add tomato pulp, mushrooms, salt, pepper, cheese, parsley and caraway seeds, stir, cook for 3 minutes more and stuff tomatoes with this mix. Add the water to your instant pot, add the steamer basket, and stuffed tomatoes inside, cover and cook on High for 4 minutes. Arrange tomatoes on a platter and serve as an appetizer. Enjoy!

Nutrition: calories 152, fat 2, fiber 4, carbs 6, protein 7

Cinnamon and Pumpkin Muffins

Preparation time: 10 minutes
Cooking time: 20 minutes
Servings: 18

Ingredients:

- 4 tablespoons ghee
- ¾ cup pumpkin puree
- 2 tablespoons flaxseed meal
- ¼ cup coconut flour
- ½ cup erythritol
- ½ teaspoon nutmeg, ground
- 1 teaspoon cinnamon powder
- ½ teaspoon baking powder
- ½ teaspoon baking soda
- 1 and ½ cups water
- 1 egg

Directions:

In a bowl, mix ghee with pumpkin puree, egg, flaxseed meal, coconut flour, erythritol, baking soda, baking powder, nutmeg and cinnamon, stir well and divide into a greased muffin pan. Add the water to your instant pot, add the steamer basket, add muffin pan inside, cover pot and cook on High for 20 minutes. Arrange muffins on a platter and serve as a snack.

Nutrition: calories 50, fat 3, fiber 1, carbs 2, protein 2

Spicy Chili Balls

Preparation time: 10 minutes
Cooking time: 5 minutes
Servings: 3

Ingredients:

- 3 bacon slices
- 1 cup water
- 3 ounces cream cheese
- ¼ teaspoon onion powder
- Salt and black pepper to the taste
- 2 jalapeno peppers, chopped
- ½ teaspoon parsley, dried
- ¼ teaspoon garlic powder

Directions:

Set your instant pot on sauté mode, add bacon, cook for a couple of minutes, transfer to paper towels drain grease and crumble it. In a bowl, mix cream cheese with jalapenos, bacon, onion, garlic powder, parsley, salt and pepper, stir well and shape balls out of this mix. Clean the pot, add the water, and the steamer basket, add spicy balls inside, cover and cook on High for 2 minutes. Arrange balls on a platter and serve as an appetizer. Enjoy!

Nutrition: calories 150, fat 5, fiber 1, carbs 2, protein 5

Italian Dip

Preparation time: 10 minutes
Cooking time: 20 minutes
Servings: 4

Ingredients:

- 4 ounces cream cheese, soft
- ½ cup mozzarella cheese
- ¼ cup coconut cream
- Salt and black pepper to the taste
- 1/2 cup tomato sauce
- 4 black olives, pitted and chopped
- ¼ cup mayonnaise
- ¼ cup parmesan cheese, grated
- 1 tablespoon green bell pepper, chopped
- 6 pepperoni slices, chopped
- ½ teaspoon Italian seasoning
- 2 cups water

Directions:

In a bowl, mix cream cheese with mozzarella, coconut cream, mayo, salt and pepper, stir and divide this into 4 ramekins. Layer tomato sauce, parmesan cheese, bell pepper, pepperoni, Italian seasoning and black olives on top, Add the water to your instant pot, add the steamer basket, add ramekins inside, cover and cook on High for 20 minutes. Serve this dip warm with veggie sticks on the side. Enjoy!

Nutrition: calories 250, fat 15, fiber 4, carbs 4, protein 12

Avocado Dip

Preparation time: 10 minutes
Cooking time: 2 minutes
Servings: 4

Ingredients:

- ¼ cup erythritol powder
- 1 cup water
- ½ cup cilantro, chopped
- 2 avocados, pitted, peeled and halved
- ¼ teaspoon stevia
- Juice from 2 limes
- Zest of 2 limes, grated
- 1 cup coconut milk

Directions:

Add the water to your instant pot, add the steamer basket, add avocado halves, cover and cook on High for 2 minutes. Transfer to your blender, add lime juice and cilantro and pulse well. Add coconut milk, lime zest, stevia and erythritol powder, pulse again, divide into bowls and serve. Enjoy!

Nutrition: calories 150, fat 6, fiber 2, carbs 4, protein 2

Minty Shrimp Appetizer

Preparation time: 10 minutes
Cooking time: 20 minutes
Servings: 16

Ingredients:

- 2 tablespoons olive oil
- 10 ounces shrimp, cooked, peeled and deveined
- 1 tablespoons mint, chopped
- 2 tablespoons erythritol
- 1/3 cup blackberries, ground
- 11 prosciutto slices
- 1/3 cup veggie stock.

Directions:

Wrap each shrimp in prosciutto slices and drizzle oil over them. In your instant pot, mix blackberries with mint, stock and erythritol, stir, set on simmer mode and cook for 2 minutes. Add steamer basket, and wrapped shrimp, cover pot and cook on High for 2 minutes. Arrange wrapped shrimp on a platter, drizzle mint sauce all over and serve. Enjoy!

Nutrition: calories 175, fat 6, fiber 2, carbs 1, protein 8

Zucchini Appetizer Salad

Preparation time: 10 minutes
Cooking time: 6 minutes
Servings: 4

Ingredients:

- 1 cup mozzarella, shredded
- ¼ cup tomato sauce
- 1 zucchini, roughly sliced
- Salt and black pepper to the taste
- A pinch of cumin, ground
- A drizzle of olive oil

Directions:

In your instant pot, mix zucchini with oil, tomato sauce, salt, pepper and cumin, toss a bit, cover and cook on High for 6 minutes. Divide between appetizer plates and serve right away. Enjoy!

Nutrition: calories 130, fat 4, fiber 2, carbs 4, protein 3

Zucchini Hummus

Preparation time: 10 minutes
Cooking time: 6 minutes
Servings: 4

Ingredients:
- 4 cups zucchini, chopped
- 3 tablespoons veggie stock
- ¼ cup olive oil
- Salt and black pepper to the taste
- 4 garlic cloves, minced
- ¾ cup sesame seeds paste
- ½ cup lemon juice
- 1 tablespoon cumin, ground

Directions:
Set your instant pot on sauté mode, add half of the oil, heat it up, add zucchini and garlic, stir and cook for 2 minutes. Add stock, salt and pepper, cover pot and cook on High for 4 minutes more. Transfer zucchini to your blender, add the rest of the oil, sesame seeds paste, lemon juice and cumin, pulse well, transfer to bowls and serve as a snack. Enjoy!

Nutrition: calories 80, fat 5, fiber 3, carbs 6, protein 7

Crab and Cheese Dip

Preparation time: 10 minutes
Cooking time: 20 minutes
Servings: 8

Ingredients:
- 8 bacon strips, sliced
- 12 ounces crab meat
- ½ cup mayonnaise
- ½ cup coconut cream
- 8 ounces cream cheese
- 2 poblano pepper, chopped
- 2 tablespoons lemon juice
- Salt and black pepper to the taste
- 4 garlic cloves, minced
- 4 green onions, minced
- 1 cup parmesan cheese, grated

Directions:
Set your instant pot on sauté mode, add bacon, cook until it's crispy, transfer to paper towels, drain grease and leave aside. In a bowl, mix coconut cream with cream cheese, mayo, half of the parmesan, poblano peppers, garlic, lemon juice, green onions, salt, pepper, crab meat and bacon and stir really well. Clean your instant pot, add crab mix, spread the rest of the parmesan on top, cover and cook on High for 14 minutes. Divide into bowls and serve as a snack. Enjoy!

Nutrition: calories 200, fat 2, fiber 2, carbs 4, protein 3

Spinach Dip

Preparation time: 10 minutes
Cooking time: 20 minutes
Servings: 6

Ingredients:

- 6 bacon slices, cooked and crumbled
- A drizzle of olive oil
- 1 tablespoon garlic, minced
- 5 ounces spinach
- 1 and ½ cups water
- ½ cup coconut cream
- 8 ounces cream cheese, soft
- 1 and ½ tablespoons parsley, chopped
- 2.5 ounces parmesan, grated
- 1 tablespoon lemon juice
- Salt and black pepper to the taste

Directions:

Set your instant pot on sauté mode, add oil heat it up, add spinach, stir, cook for 1 minute and transfer to a bowl. Add cream cheese, garlic, salt, pepper, coconut cream, parsley, bacon, lemon juice and parmesan, stir well and divide this into 6 ramekins. Add the water to your instant pot, add steamer basket, add ramekins inside, cover and cook on High for 15 minutes. Introduce in a preheated broiler for 4 minutes and serve right away. Enjoy!

Nutrition: calories 255, fat 7, fiber 3, carbs 5, protein 7

Stuffed Mushrooms

Preparation time: 10 minutes
Cooking time: 15 minutes
Servings: 5

Ingredients:

- ¼ cup mayo
- 1 teaspoon garlic powder
- 1 small yellow onion, chopped
- 24 ounces white mushroom caps
- 1 and ½ cups water
- Salt and black pepper to the taste
- 1 teaspoon curry powder
- 4 ounces cream cheese, soft
- ¼ cup coconut cream
- ½ cup Mexican cheese, shredded
- 1 cup shrimp, cooked, peeled, deveined and chopped

Directions:

In a bowl, mix mayo with garlic powder, onion, curry powder, cream cheese, cream, Mexican cheese, shrimp, salt and pepper, stir and stuff mushrooms with this mix. Add the water to your instant pot, add steamer basket, add mushrooms inside, cover pot and cook on High for 14 minutes. Arrange mushrooms on a platter and serve as an appetizer. Enjoy!

Nutrition: calories 244, fat 16, fiber 3, carbs 7, protein 12

Turkey Meatballs

Preparation time: 10 minutes
Cooking time: 6 minutes
Servings: 16

Ingredients:

- 1 egg
- Salt and black pepper to the taste
- ¼ cup coconut flour
- 2 tablespoons sun-dried tomatoes, chopped
- 1 pound turkey meat, ground
- ½ teaspoon garlic powder
- ½ cup mozzarella cheese, shredded
- 2 tablespoons olive oil
- ¼ cup tomato paste
- 2 tablespoon basil, chopped

Directions:

In a bowl, mix turkey with salt, pepper, egg, flour, garlic powder, sun-dried tomatoes, mozzarella and basil, stir well and shape 12 meatballs out of this mix. Set your instant pot on sauté mode, add oil, heat it up, add meatballs, stir and brown for 2 minutes on each side. Add tomato paste over them, toss a bit, cover and cook on High for 8 minutes. Arrange meatballs on a platter and serve them right away. Enjoy!

Nutrition: calories 100, fat 6, fiber 3, carbs 5, protein 3

Italian Chicken Wings

Preparation time: 10 minutes
Cooking time: 27 minutes
Servings: 6

Ingredients:

- 6-pound chicken wings, cut into halves
- 2 cups water
- Salt and black pepper to the taste
- ½ teaspoon Italian seasoning
- 2 tablespoons ghee
- ½ cup parmesan cheese, grated
- A pinch of red pepper flakes, crushed
- 1 teaspoon garlic powder
- 1 egg

Directions:

Put the water in your instant pot, add the trivet, add chicken wings, cover and cook on High for 7 minutes. Meanwhile, in your blender, mix ghee with cheese, egg, salt, pepper, pepper flakes, garlic powder and Italian seasoning and blend very well. Arrange chicken wings on a lined baking sheet, pour cheese sauce over them, introduce in preheated broiler and broil for 5 minutes. Flip and broil for 5 minutes more, arrange them all on a platter and serve. Enjoy!

Nutrition: calories 134, fat 5, fiber 1, carbs 2, protein 7

Zucchini Rolls

Preparation time: 10 minutes
Cooking time: 7 minutes
Servings: 24

Ingredients:

- 2 tablespoons olive oil
- 3 zucchinis, thinly sliced
- 24 basil leaves
- 2 tablespoons mint, chopped
- 1 and ½ cups water
- 1 and 1/3 cup ricotta cheese
- Salt and black pepper to the taste
- ¼ cup basil, chopped
- Tomato sauce for serving

Directions:

Set your instant pot on sauté mode, add zucchini slices, drizzle the oil over them, season with salt and pepper, cook for 2 minutes on each side and transfer to a plate. In a bowl, mix ricotta with chopped basil, mint, salt and pepper, stir, divide this into zucchini slices and roll them. Add the water to your instant pot, add steamer basket, add zucchini rolls inside, cover and cook on High for 3 minutes. Arrange on a platter and serve with tomato sauce on the side. Enjoy!

Nutrition: calories 70, fat 3, fiber 1, carbs 2, protein 4

Spicy Salsa

Preparation time: 10 minutes
Cooking time: 3 minutes
Servings: 4

Ingredients:

- 1 red onion, chopped
- 2 tablespoons lime juice
- 2 avocados, pitted, peeled and chopped
- 3 jalapeno pepper, chopped
- Salt and black pepper to the taste
- 2 tablespoons cumin powder
- ½ tomato, chopped

Directions:

In your instant pot, mix onion with avocados, peppers, salt, black pepper, cumin, lime juice and tomato, stir, cover and cook on Low for 3 minutes. Divide into bowls and serve. Enjoy!

Nutrition: calories 120, fat 2, fiber 2, carbs 5, protein 4

Salmon Balls

Preparation time: 10 minutes
Cooking time: 10 minutes
Servings: 4

Ingredients:

- 2 tablespoons ghee
- 2 garlic cloves, minced
- 1/3 cup onion, chopped
- 1 pound wild salmon, boneless, skinless and minced
- ¼ cup chives, chopped
- 1 egg
- 2 tablespoons Dijon mustard
- 1 tablespoon coconut flour
- Salt and black pepper to the taste

For the coconut sauce:

- 4 garlic cloves, minced
- 2 tablespoons ghee
- 2 tablespoons Dijon mustard
- Juice and zest of 1 lemon
- 2 cups coconut cream
- 2 tablespoons chives, chopped

Directions:

Set your instant pot on sauté mode, add 2 tablespoons ghee, heat it up, add onion and 2 garlic cloves, stir, cook for 3 minutes and transfer to a bowl. Add salmon, chives, coconut flour, salt, pepper, 2 tablespoons mustard and egg, stir and shape medium balls out of this mix. Set the pot on sauté mode again, add 2 tablespoons ghee, heat it up, add 4 garlic cloves, stir and cook for 1 minute. Add coconut cream, 2 tablespoons Dijon mustard, lemon juice and zest and chives, stir, drop salmon balls into this sauce, cover pot, cook on High for 6 minutes, arrange on a platter and serve. Enjoy!

Nutrition: calories 171, fat 5, fiber 1, carbs 6, protein 23

Delicious Oysters

Preparation time: 10 minutes
Cooking time: 6 minutes
Servings: 3

Ingredients:

- 6 big oysters, shucked
- 1 and ½ cups water
- 3 garlic cloves, minced
- 1 lemon cut into wedges
- 1 tablespoon parsley
- A pinch of sweet paprika
- 2 tablespoons melted ghee

Directions:

Divide ghee, parsley, paprika and garlic in each oyster. Add the water to your instant pot, add steamer basket, add oysters, cover pot and cook on High for 6 minutes. Arrange oysters on a platter and serve with lemon wedges on the side. Enjoy!

Nutrition: calories 90, fat 1, fiber 1, carbs 2, protein 4

Tuna Patties

Preparation time: 10 minutes
Cooking time: 8 minutes
Servings: 12

Ingredients:

- 15 ounces canned tuna, drained and flaked
- 3 eggs
- ½ teaspoon dill, chopped
- 1 teaspoon parsley, dried
- ½ cup red onion, chopped
- 1 and ½ cups water
- 1 teaspoon garlic powder
- Salt and black pepper to the taste
- A drizzle of olive oil

Directions:

In a bowl, mix tuna with salt, pepper, dill, parsley, onion, garlic powder and eggs, stir and shape medium patties out of this mix. Set your instant pot on sauté mode, add a drizzle of oil, heat it up, add tuna patties, cook them for 2 minutes on each side and transfer to a plate. Clean the pot, add the water, add steamer basket, add tuna cakes, cover pot and cook on High for 4 minutes. Arrange patties on a platter and serve. Enjoy!

Nutrition: calories 140, fat 2, fiber 1, carbs 0.6, protein 6

Worcestershire Shrimp

Preparation time: 10 minutes
Cooking time: 8 minutes
Servings: 2

Ingredients:

- ½ pound big shrimp, peeled and deveined
- 2 teaspoons Worcestershire sauce
- 2 teaspoons olive oil
- Juice of 1 lemon
- Salt and black pepper to the taste
- 1 teaspoon Creole seasoning

Directions:

In your instant pot, mix shrimp with Worcestershire sauce, oil, lemon juice, salt, pepper and seasoning, stir, cover and cook on High for 4 minutes. Arrange shrimp on a lined baking sheet, introduce in preheated broiler and broil for 4 minutes more. Arrange on a platter and serve. Enjoy!

Nutrition: calories 120, fat 3, fiber 1, carbs 6, protein 5

Ketogenic Instant Pot Side Dish Recipes

Napa Cabbage Side Salad

Preparation time: 40 minutes
Cooking time: 5 minutes
Servings: 6

Ingredients:

- Salt and black pepper to the taste
- 1 pound napa cabbage, chopped
- 1 carrot, julienned
- 2 tablespoons veggie stock
- ½ cup daikon radish
- 3 garlic cloves, minced
- 3 green onion stalks, chopped
- 1 tablespoon coconut aminos
- 3 tablespoons chili flakes
- 1 tablespoon olive oil
- ½ inch ginger, grated

Directions:

In a bowl, mix cabbage with salt and black pepper, massage well for 10 minutes, cover and leave aside for 30 minutes. In another bowl, mix chili flakes with aminos, garlic, oil and ginger and stir whisk well. Drain cabbage well, transfer to your instant pot, add stock, carrots, green onions, radish and the chili paste you made, stir, cover and cook on High for 5 minutes. Divide between plates and serve as a side dish. Enjoy!

Nutrition: calories 100, fat 3, fiber 4, carbs 5, protein 2

Asian Brussels Sprouts

Preparation time: 10 minutes
Cooking time: 4 minutes
Servings: 4

Ingredients:

- 1 pound Brussels sprouts, halved
- 3 tablespoons chicken stock
- Salt and black pepper to the taste
- 1 teaspoon sesame seeds, toasted
- 1 tablespoon green onions, chopped
- 1 and ½ tablespoons stevia
- 1 tablespoon coconut aminos
- 2 tablespoons olive oil
- 1 tablespoon keto sriracha sauce

Directions:

In a bowl, mix oil with coconut aminos, sriracha, stevia, salt and black pepper and whisk well. Put Brussels sprouts in your instant pot; add sriracha mix, stock, green onions and sesame seeds, stir, cover and cook on High for 4 minutes. Divide between plates and serve as a side dish. Enjoy!

Nutrition: calories 110, fat 4, fiber 2, carbs 4, protein 2

Cauliflower and Parmesan

Preparation time: 10 minutes
Cooking time: 4 minutes
Servings: 6

Ingredients:
- 1 cauliflower head, florets separated
- ½ cup veggie stock
- 2 garlic cloves, minced
- Salt and black pepper to the taste
- 1/3 cup parmesan, grated
- 1 tablespoon parsley, chopped
- 3 tablespoons olive oil

Directions:
In a bowl, mix oil with garlic, salt, pepper and cauliflower florets, toss and transfer to your instant pot. Add stock, cover pot and cook on High for 4 minutes. Add parsley and parmesan, toss, divide between plates and serve as a side dish. Enjoy!

Nutrition: calories 120, fat 2, fiber 3, carbs 5, protein 3

Swiss Chard and Garlic

Preparation time: 10 minutes
Cooking time: 6 minutes
Servings: 2

Ingredients:
- 2 tablespoons ghee
- 3 tablespoons lemon juice
- ½ cup chicken stock
- 4 bacon slices, chopped
- 1 bunch Swiss chard, roughly chopped
- ½ teaspoon garlic paste
- Salt and black pepper to the taste

Directions:
Set your instant pot on sauté mode, add bacon, stir and cook for a couple of minutes. Add ghee, lemon juice and garlic paste and stir. Add Swiss chard, salt, pepper and stock, cover pot and cook on High for 3 minutes. Divide between plates and serve as a side dish. Enjoy!

Nutrition: calories 160, fat 7, fiber 3, carbs 6, protein 4

Mushroom and Arugula Side Dish

Preparation time: 10 minutes
Cooking time: 5 minutes
Servings: 4

Ingredients:

- 2 tablespoons ghee
- Salt and black pepper to the taste
- 1 pound cremini mushrooms, chopped
- 4 tablespoons veggie stock
- 4 bunches arugula
- 8 slices prosciutto, chopped
- 2 tablespoons balsamic vinegar
- 8 sun-dried tomatoes in oil, chopped
- 1 tablespoon parsley, chopped

Directions:

Set your instant pot on sauté mode, add prosciutto, stir and cook for 2 minutes. Add ghee, melt it, add mushrooms, salt and pepper, stir and cook for 2 minutes. Add vinegar, stock and tomatoes, stir, cover and cook on High for 3 minutes. Add parsley, stir and transfer this mix to a bowl. Add arugula, toss, divide between plates and serve as a side dish. Enjoy!

Nutrition: calories 200, fat 3, fiber 2, carbs 5, protein 6

Red Chard and Olives

Preparation time: 10 minutes
Cooking time: 5 minutes
Servings: 4

Ingredients:

- 2 tablespoons olive oil
- 1 bunch red chard, roughly chopped
- 3 tablespoons veggie stock
- 2 tablespoons capers
- 1 yellow onion, chopped
- Juice of 1 lemon
- Salt and black pepper to the taste
- 1 teaspoon stevia
- ¼ cup kalamata olives, pitted and chopped

Directions:

Set your instant pot on sauté mode, add oil, heat it up, add onion, stir and cook for 2 minutes. Add stevia, olives, chard, salt, pepper and stock, stir, cover and cook on High for 3 minutes. Add capers and lemon juice, stir, divide between plates and serve as a side dish. Enjoy!

Nutrition: calories 123, fat 4, fiber 3, carbs 4, protein 5

Kale and Almonds

Preparation time: 10 minutes
Cooking time: 7 minutes
Servings: 4

Ingredients:
- 1 cup water
- 1 big kale bunch, roughly chopped
- 1 tablespoon balsamic vinegar
- 1/3 cup almonds, toasted
- 3 garlic cloves, minced
- 1 small yellow onion, chopped
- 2 tablespoons olive oil

Directions:

Set your instant pot on sauté mode, add oil, heat it up, add onion, stir and cook for 3 minutes. Add garlic, water and kale, stir, cover and cook on High for 4 minutes. Add salt, pepper, vinegar and almonds, toss well, divide between plates and serve as a side dish. Enjoy!

Nutrition: calories 140, fat 6, fiber 3, carbs 5, protein 3

Green Cabbage and Paprika

Preparation time: 10 minutes
Cooking time: 7 minutes
Servings: 4

Ingredients:
- 1 and ½ pound green cabbage, shredded
- Salt and black pepper to the taste
- 3 tablespoons ghee
- 1 cup veggie stock
- ¼ teaspoon sweet paprika

Directions:

Set your instant pot on sauté mode, add ghee, melt it, add cabbage, salt, pepper and stock, stir, cover and cook on High for 7 minutes. Add paprika, toss a bit, divide between plates and serve as a side dish. Enjoy!

Nutrition: calories 170, fat 4, fiber 2, carbs 5, protein 5

Coconut Cream and Sausage Gravy

Preparation time: 10 minutes
Cooking time: 7 minutes
Servings: 4

Ingredients:
- 4 ounces sausages, minced
- Salt and black pepper to the taste
- 1 cup coconut cream
- 2 tablespoons ghee
- ½ teaspoon stevia

Directions:
Set your instant pot on sauté mode, add minced sausage, stir and cook for a couple of minutes. Add ghee, cream, stevia, salt and pepper, stir, cover and cook on High for 5 minutes. Serve this with a steak. Enjoy!

Nutrition: calories 125, fat 7, fiber 1, carbs 5, protein 4

Vietnamese Eggplant Side Dish

Preparation time: 10 minutes
Cooking time: 10 minutes
Servings: 4

Ingredients:
- 1 big eggplant, roughly chopped
- 1 yellow onion, chopped
- 2 tablespoons olive oil
- 2 teaspoons chili paste

For the sauce:
- 1 teaspoon stevia
- ½ cup chicken stock
- 2 teaspoons garlic, minced
- ½ cup water
- 3 tablespoons coconut milk
- 4 green onions, chopped

- 2 tablespoons coconut aminos

Directions:
Set your instant pot on sauté mode, add oil, heat it up, add eggplant and brown for a couple of minutes. Add yellow onion, garlic, water, chili paste and coconut milk and stir. Heat up a pan with the chicken stock over medium heat, add stevia and aminos, stir, cook for a couple of minutes and transfer to the instant pot as well. Cover your instant pot and cook on High for 4 minutes. Add green onions as well, stir, divide between plates and serve as a side dish. Enjoy!

Nutrition: calories 182, fat 3, fiber 4, carbs 7, protein 4

Baby Mushrooms Sauté

Preparation time: 10 minutes
Cooking time: 10 minutes
Servings: 4

Ingredients:
- 4 tablespoons ghee
- 3 tablespoons veggie stock
- 1 teaspoon garlic powder
- 16 ounces baby mushrooms
- Salt and black pepper to the taste
- 3 tablespoons onion, dried
- 3 tablespoons parsley flakes

Directions:
In a bowl, mix parsley flakes with onion, salt, pepper, garlic powder and mushrooms and toss well. Set your instant pot on sauté mode, add ghee, melt it, add mushrooms mix, stir and cook for 3-4 minutes. Add stock, cover pot and cook on High for 6 minutes. Divide between plates and serve as a side dish. Enjoy!

Nutrition: calories 172, fat 6, fiber 5, carbs 6, protein 2

Cauliflower and Eggs Salad

Preparation time: 10 minutes
Cooking time: 5 minutes
Servings: 10

Ingredients:
- 21 ounces cauliflower, florets separated
- 1 cup red onion, chopped
- 1 cup celery, chopped
- ½ cup water
- Salt and black pepper to the taste
- 2 tablespoons balsamic vinegar
- 1 teaspoon stevia
- 4 eggs, hard-boiled, peeled and chopped
- 1 cup mayonnaise

Directions:
Put the water in your instant pot, add steamer basket, add cauliflower, cover pot and cook on High for 5 minutes. Transfer cauliflower to a bowl, add eggs, celery and onion and toss. In a separate bowl, mix mayo with salt, pepper, vinegar and stevia and whisk well. Add this to your salad, toss, divide between plates and serve as a side dish. Enjoy!

Nutrition: calories 171, fat 6, fiber 2, carbs 6, protein 3

Asparagus and Cheese Side Dish

Preparation time: 10 minutes
Cooking time: 6 minutes
Servings: 4

Ingredients:
- 10 ounces asparagus, cut into medium pieces
- Salt and black pepper to the taste
- 2 tablespoons parmesan, grated
- 1/3 cup Monterey jack cheese, shredded
- 2 tablespoons mustard
- 2 ounces cream cheese
- 1/3 cup coconut cream
- 3 tablespoons bacon, cooked and crumbled

Directions

In your instant pot, mix asparagus with salt, pepper, parmesan, Monterey jack cheese, mustard, cream cheese, coconut cream and bacon, stir, cover and cook on High for 6 minutes. Divide between plates and serve as a side dish. Enjoy!

Nutrition: calories 156, fat 3, fiber 2, carbs 5, protein 7

Sprouts and Apple Side Dish

Preparation time: 10 minutes
Cooking time: 7 minutes
Servings: 4

Ingredients:
- 1 green apple, cored and julienned
- 1 and ½ teaspoons olive oil
- 4 cups alfalfa sprouts
- Salt and black pepper to the taste
- ¼ cup coconut milk

Directions:

Set your instant pot on sauté mode, add oil, heat it up, add apple and sprouts, stir, cover pot and cook on High for 5 minutes. Add salt, pepper and coconut milk, stir, cover pot again and cook on High for 2 minutes more. Divide between plates and serve as a side dish. Enjoy!

Nutrition: calories 120, fat 3, fiber 1, carbs 3, protein 3

Radishes and Chives

Preparation time: 10 minutes
Cooking time: 7 minutes
Servings: 2

Ingredients:
- 2 cups radishes, cut into quarters
- ½ cup chicken stock
- Salt and black pepper to the taste
- 2 tablespoons ghee, melted
- 1 tablespoon chives, chopped
- 1 tablespoon lemon zest, grated

Directions:
In your instant pot, mix radishes with stock, salt, pepper and lemon zest, stir, cover pot and cook on High for 7 minutes. Add melted ghee, toss a bit, divide between plates, sprinkle chives on top and serve as a side dish. Enjoy!

Nutrition: calories 102, fat 4, fiber 1, carbs 6, protein 5

Hot Radishes with Bacon and Cheese

Preparation time: 10 minutes
Cooking time: 10 minutes
Servings: 1

Ingredients:
- 7 ounces red radishes, halved
- ½ cup veggie stock
- 2 tablespoons coconut cream
- 2 bacon slices, chopped
- 1 tablespoon green onion, chopped
- 1 tablespoon cheddar cheese, grated
- Hot sauce to the taste
- Salt and black pepper to the taste

Directions:
Set your instant pot on sauté mode, add bacon, stir and cook for a couple of minutes. Add radishes, salt, pepper and stock, stir, cover and cook on High for 4 minutes. Add green onion, cream, cheese and hot sauce, stir, cover the pot again and cook on High for 2 minutes more. Divide between plates and serve as a side dish. Enjoy!

Nutrition: calories 170, fat 16, fiber 3, carbs 6, protein 12

Avocado Side Salad

Preparation time: 10 minutes
Cooking time: 7 minutes
Servings: 4

Ingredients:
- 4 cups mixed lettuce leaves, torn
- 4 eggs
- 2 cups water
- 2 teaspoons mustard
- 1 avocado, pitted and sliced
- ¼ cup mayonnaise
- 2 garlic cloves, minced
- 1 tablespoon chives, chopped
- Salt and black pepper to the taste

Directions:
Put the water in your instant pot, add steamer basket, add eggs inside, cover pot, cook on High for 7 minutes, cool them down, chop and transfer to a bowl. Add lettuce, avocado, garlic, chives, salt and pepper and toss. In a small bowl, mix mustard with mayo, salt and pepper, whisk well, add to salad, toss to coat and serve as a side salad. Enjoy!

Nutrition: calories 134, fat 7, fiber 4, carbs 7, protein 10

Swiss Chard and Pine Nuts

Preparation time: 10 minutes
Cooking time: 5 minutes
Servings: 4

Ingredients:
- 1 bunch Swiss chard, cut into strips
- 2 tablespoons olive oil
- 1 tablespoon balsamic vinegar
- 1 small yellow onion, chopped
- ¼ teaspoon red pepper flakes
- ¼ cup pine nuts, toasted
- ¼ cup raisins
- 1 tablespoon balsamic vinegar
- Salt and black pepper to the taste

Directions:
Set your instant pot on sauté mode, add oil, heat it up, add onion and chard, stir and cook for 2 minutes. Add pepper flakes, salt, pepper and vinegar, stir, cover and cook on High for 3 minutes. Add raisins and pine nuts, toss, divide between plates and serve as a side dish. Enjoy!

Nutrition: calories 120, fat 2, fiber 1, carbs 2, protein 4

Spinach and Chard Mix

Preparation time: 10 minutes
Cooking time: 6 minutes
Servings: 4

Ingredients:

- 1 apple, cored and chopped
- 1 yellow onion, sliced
- 4 tablespoons pine nuts, toasted
- 3 tablespoons olive oil
- ¼ cup raisins
- 6 garlic cloves, chopped
- ¼ cup balsamic vinegar
- 2 and ½ cups baby spinach
- 2 and ½ cups Swiss chard, roughly torn
- Salt and black pepper to the taste
- A pinch of nutmeg

Directions:

Set your instant pot on sauté mode, add oil, heat it up, add onion and apple, stir and cook for 3 minutes. Add garlic, raisins, spinach, chard and vinegar, stir, cover and cook on High for 3 minutes. Add salt, pepper, nutmeg and pine nuts, stir, divide between plates and serve as a side dish. Enjoy!

Nutrition: calories 140, fat 1, fiber 2, carbs 3, protein 3

Cherry Tomatoes and Parmesan Mix

Preparation time: 10 minutes
Cooking time: 7 minutes
Servings: 8

Ingredients:

- 1 jalapeno pepper, chopped
- 4 garlic cloves, minced
- Salt and black pepper to the taste
- 2 pounds cherry tomatoes, cut into halves
- 1 yellow onion, cut into wedges
- ¼ cup olive oil
- ½ teaspoon oregano, dried
- 1 and ½ cups chicken stock
- ¼ cup basil, chopped
- ½ cup parmesan, grated

Directions:

Set your instant pot on sauté mode, add oil, heat it up, add onion and garlic, stir and cook for 2-3 minutes. Add jalapeno, tomatoes, oregano, salt, pepper and stock, stir, cover and cook on High for 4 minutes. Add basil and parmesan, toss a bit, divide between plates and serve as a side dish. Enjoy!

Nutrition: calories 120, fat 2, fiber 3, carbs 5, protein 4

Almond Cauliflower Rice

Preparation time: 10 minutes
Cooking time: 7 minutes
Servings: 4

Ingredients:

- ½ cup yellow onion, finely chopped
- 1 tablespoon ghee
- 1 celery stalk, chopped
- 1 and ½ cups cauliflower rice
- 4 ounces chicken stock
- Salt and black pepper to the taste
- ½ cup almonds, toasted and chopped
- 2 tablespoons parsley, chopped

Directions:

Set your instant pot on Sauté mode, add ghee, melt it, add celery and onion, stir and sauté for 3 minutes. Add cauliflower, salt, pepper and stock, stir, cover and cook on High for 4 minutes. Add parsley and almonds, toss, divide between plates and serve as a side dish. Enjoy!

Nutrition: calories 172, fat 3, fiber 5, carbs 7, protein 12

Saffron Cauliflower Rice

Preparation time: 10 minutes
Cooking time: 7 minutes
Servings: 6

Ingredients:

- 2 tablespoons olive oil
- ½ teaspoon saffron threads, crushed
- ½ cup onion, chopped
- 2 tablespoons coconut milk
- 1 and ½ cups cauliflower rice
- 2 cups veggie stock
- Salt and black pepper to the taste
- 1 tablespoon stevia
- 1 cinnamon stick
- 1/3 cup almonds, chopped

Directions:

In a bowl, mix milk with saffron and stir. Set your instant pot on sauté mode, add oil, heat it up, add onion, stir and cook for 2 minutes. Add cauliflower rice, stock, saffron mix, stevia, almonds, salt, pepper and cinnamon, stir, cover and cook on High for 5 minutes. Stir your rice one more time, discard cinnamon, divide between plates and serve as a side dish. Enjoy!

Nutrition: calories 162, fat 4, fiber 3, carbs 7, protein 4

Hot Cauliflower Rice and Avocado

Preparation time: 10 minutes
Cooking time: 4 minutes
Servings: 8

Ingredients:
- 1 cup cauliflower rice
- 1 and ¼ cups veggie stock
- ¼ cup green hot sauce
- ½ cup cilantro, chopped
- ½ avocado, pitted, peeled and chopped
- Salt and black pepper to the taste

Directions:
In your instant pot, mix cauliflower rice with stock, salt and pepper, stir, cover and cook on High for 4 minutes. In your blender, mix avocado with hot sauce and cilantro, pulse well and add to cauliflower rice. Stir everything, divide between plates and serve as a side dish. Enjoy!

Nutrition: calories 154, fat 1, fiber 2, carbs 5, protein 7

Celery and Rosemary Side Dish

Preparation time: 10 minutes
Cooking time: 6 minutes
Servings: 4

Ingredients:
- 1 pound celery, peeled and cubed
- 1 cup water
- 2 garlic cloves, minced
- Salt and black pepper to the taste
- ¼ teaspoon rosemary, dried
- 1 tablespoon olive oil

Directions:
Put the water in your instant pot, add steamer basket, add celery cubes inside, cover pot and cook on High for 4 minutes. In a bowl, mix oil with garlic and rosemary and whisk well. Add steamed celery, toss well, spread on a lined baking sheet and introduce in a preheated broiler for 3 minutes. Divide between plates and serve as a side dish. Enjoy!

Nutrition: calories 100, fat 3, fiber 3, carbs 8, protein 3

Lemon Cauliflower Rice

Preparation time: 10 minutes
Cooking time: 10 minutes
Servings: 6

Ingredients:

- 1 and ½ cup cauliflower rice
- 2 tablespoons ghee
- 1 tablespoon olive oil
- 1 yellow onion, chopped
- 2 tablespoons lemon juice
- 1 teaspoon lemon zest, grated
- 2 cups chicken stock
- 2 tablespoons parsley, chopped
- Salt and black pepper to the taste
- 2 tablespoons parmesan, grated

Directions:

Set your instant pot on sauté mode, add ghee and oil, heat them up, add onion, stir and sauté them for 3 minutes. Add cauliflower rice, stock, lemon juice, salt and pepper, stir, cover and cook on High for 4 minutes. Add parmesan, lemon zest and parsley, stir well, cover pot and leave aside for 3 minutes more. Divide between plates and serve as a side dish. Enjoy!

Nutrition: calories 172, fat 3, fiber 3, carbs 4, protein 3

Spinach Cauliflower Rice

Preparation time: 10 minutes
Cooking time: 8 minutes
Servings: 6

Ingredients:

- 2 garlic cloves, minced
- 2 tablespoons olive oil
- ¾ cup yellow onion, chopped
- 1 and ½ cups cauliflower rice
- 12 ounces spinach, chopped
- 2 and ½ cups hot veggie stock
- Salt and black pepper to the taste
- 4 ounces goat cheese, crumbled
- 2 tablespoons lemon juice

Directions:

Set your instant pot on sauté mode, add oil, heat it up, add onion and garlic, stir and cook for 2 minutes. Add cauliflower rice, stock, salt and pepper, cover and cook on High for 4 minutes. Add lemon juice and spinach, stir, cover and cook on High for 2 minutes more. Add goat cheese, stir your rice, divide between plates and serve as a side dish. Enjoy!

Nutrition: calories 210, fat 4, fiber 4, carbs 6, protein 8

Squash Puree

Preparation time: 10 minutes
Cooking time: 20 minutes
Servings: 4

Ingredients:
- ½ cup water
- 2 acorn squash, cut into halves and seeded
- Salt and black pepper to the taste
- ¼ teaspoon baking soda
- 2 tablespoons ghee, melted
- ½ teaspoon nutmeg, grated
- 2 tablespoons stevia

Directions:
Add the water to your instant pot, add the steamer basket, add squash halves, season them with salt, pepper and baking soda, cover pot and cook on High for 20 minutes. Scrape squash flesh, transfer to a bowl, Add salt, pepper, ghee, nutmeg and stevia, mash well, divide between plates and serve as a side dish. Enjoy!

Nutrition: calories 152, fat 3, fiber 2, carbs 4, protein 3

Celeriac Fries

Preparation time: 10 minutes
Cooking time: 10 minutes
Servings: 4

Ingredients:
- 2 big celeriac, peeled and cut into medium wedges
- 1 cup water
- Salt to the taste
- ¼ teaspoon baking soda
- Olive oil for frying

Directions:
Put the water in your instant pot, add salt and the baking soda, and the steamer basket, add celeriac fries inside, cover, cook on High for 4 minutes, drain and transfer them to a bowl. Heat up a pan with some olive oil over medium high heat, add celeriac fries, cook until they are gold on all sides, drain grease, transfer them to plates and serve as a side dish. Enjoy!

Nutrition: calories 182, fat 5, fiber 5, carbs 7, protein 10

Green Beans Side Dish

Preparation time: 10 minutes
Cooking time: 10 minutes
Servings: 4

Ingredients:

- 1 pound fresh green beans, trimmed
- 1 small yellow onion, chopped
- 6 ounces bacon, chopped
- 1 garlic clove, minced
- 8 ounces mushrooms, sliced
- Salt and black pepper to the taste
- A splash of balsamic vinegar

Directions:

Put green beans in your instant pot, add water to cover them, cover the pot, cook at High for 3 minutes, drain and transfer them to a bowl. Clean your instant pot, set on sauté mode, add bacon, stir and cook for 2 minutes. Add onion, mushroom and garlic, stir and cook for 3 minutes more. Return green beans to the pot, add salt, pepper and vinegar, toss well, divide between plates and serve as a side dish. Enjoy!

Nutrition: calories 152, fat 6, fiber 3, carbs 6, protein 6

Cauliflower and Pineapple Risotto

Preparation time: 10 minutes
Cooking time: 6 minutes
Servings: 6

Ingredients:

- 2 cups cauliflower rice
- 3 cups water
- ¼ teaspoon sweet paprika
- ½ pineapple, peeled and chopped
- Salt and black pepper to the taste
- 2 teaspoons olive oil

Directions:

In your instant pot, mix cauliflower rice with pineapple, water, oil, salt and pepper, stir, cover and cook on High for 6 minutes. Add paprika and more salt and pepper if needed, toss a bit, divide between plates and serve as a side dish. Enjoy!

Nutrition: calories 162, fat 4, fiber 3, carbs 6, protein 6

Parsnips Mash

Preparation time: 10 minutes
Cooking time: 10 minutes
Servings: 4

Ingredients:
- 2 and ½ pounds parsnips, chopped
- 4 tablespoons ghee, melted
- Salt and black pepper to the taste
- 1 and ½ cups beef stock
- 1 thyme sprigs, chopped
- 1 yellow onion, roughly chopped

Directions:
Set your instant pot on Sauté mode, add 3 tablespoons ghee, melt it, add onion, stir and cook for 3 minutes. Add parsnips, stir and cook for 3 minutes more. Add thyme and stock, cover pot and cook on High for 4 minutes. Transfer this to your blender, add the rest of the ghee, pulse well, divide between plates and serve as a side dish. Enjoy!

Nutrition: calories 152, fat 3, fiber 3, carbs 6, protein 8

Cauliflower Mash

Preparation time: 10 minutes
Cooking time: 6 minutes
Servings: 4

Ingredients:
- 1 cauliflower, florets separated
- Salt and black pepper to the taste
- 1 and ½ cups water
- ½ teaspoon turmeric, ground
- 1 tablespoon ghee, melted
- 3 chives, chopped

Directions:
Put the water in your instant pot, add the steamer basket, add cauliflower inside, cover and cook on High for 6 minutes. Transfer cauliflower to a bowl, mash using a potato masher, add melted ghee, turmeric, salt and pepper and whisk really well. Divide between plates and serve as a side dish with chives sprinkled on top. Enjoy!

Nutrition: calories 100, fat 3, fiber 2, carbs 5, protein 5

Turnips Puree

Preparation time: 10 minutes
Cooking time: 5 minutes
Servings: 4

Ingredients:

- 4 turnips, peeled and chopped
- ½ cup chicken stock
- Salt and black pepper to the taste
- 1 yellow onion, chopped
- ¼ cup coconut cream

Directions:

In your instant pot, mix turnips with stock and onion, stir, cover, cook on High for 5 minutes, blend using an immersion blender and transfer to a bowl. Add salt, pepper and cream blend again with your immersion blender, divide between plates and serve as a side dish. Enjoy!

Nutrition: calories 100, fat 3, fiber 3, carbs 7, protein 3

Carrot Mash

Preparation time: 5 minutes
Cooking time: 4 minutes
Servings: 4

Ingredients:

- 1 and ½ pounds carrots, peeled and chopped
- 1 tablespoon ghee, melted
- Salt and white pepper to the taste
- 1 cup water
- 1 tablespoon stevia

Directions:

Put carrots in your instant pot, add water, cover, cook at High for 4 minutes, drain, transfer to a bowl and mash using an immersion blender. Add ghee, salt, pepper and stevia, blend again, divide between plates and serve as a side dish. Enjoy!

Nutrition: calories 100, fat 3, fiber 2, carbs 5, protein 2

Carrots with Thyme and Dill

Preparation time: 10 minutes
Cooking time; 5 minutes
Servings: 4

Ingredients:
- ½ cup water
- 1 pound baby carrots
- 3 tablespoons stevia
- 1 tablespoon thyme, chopped
- 1 tablespoon dill, chopped
- Salt to the taste
- 2 tablespoons ghee

Directions:
Put the water in your instant pot, add the steamer basket, add carrots inside, cover, cook on High for 3 minutes, drain and transfer to a bowl. Set your instant pot on Sauté mode, add ghee, melt it, add stevia, thyme, dill and return carrots as well. Stir, cook for a couple of minutes, divide between plates and serve as a side dish. Enjoy!

Nutrition: calories 162, fat 4, fiber 4, carbs 8, protein 3

Lemon Broccoli

Preparation time: 5 minutes
Cooking time: 15 minutes
Servings: 6

Ingredients:
- 31 oz broccoli, florets separated
- 1 cup water
- 5 lemon slices
- Salt and black pepper to the taste

Directions:
Pour the water in your instant pot, add broccoli, salt, pepper and lemon slices, cover and cook on High for 15 minutes. Drain broccoli, divide between plates, season with more salt and pepper and serve as a side dish. Enjoy!

Nutrition: calories 82, fat 1, fiber 2, carbs 6, protein 3

Poached Fennel

Preparation time: 5 minutes
Cooking time: 6 minutes
Servings: 3

Ingredients:
- 2 big fennel bulbs, sliced
- 2 tablespoons ghee
- 1 tablespoon coconut flour
- 2 cups coconut milk
- ¼ teaspoon nutmeg, ground
- Salt and black pepper to the taste.

Directions:
Set your instant pot on Sauté mode, add ghee, melt it, add fennel, stir and cook for 2 minutes. Add coconut flour, salt, pepper, milk and nutmeg, stir, cover and cook on High for 4 minutes. Divide poached fennel between plates and serve as a side dish. Enjoy!

Nutrition: calories 121, fat 2, fiber 3, carbs 6, protein 3

Mixed Bell Peppers Side Dish

Preparation time: 10 minutes
Cooking time: 8 minutes
Servings: 4

Ingredients:
- 2 yellow bell peppers, thinly sliced
- 1 green bell pepper, thinly sliced
- 2 red bell peppers, thinly sliced
- 2 tomatoes, chopped
- 2 garlic cloves, minced
- 1 red onion, thinly sliced
- Salt and black pepper to the taste
- 1 bunch parsley, finely chopped
- A drizzle of olive oil

Directions:
Set your instant pot on Sauté mode, add oil, heat it up, add onion, stir and cook for 2 minutes, Add red, yellow and green peppers, tomatoes, salt and pepper, stir, cover and cook at High for 6 minutes. Add garlic and parsley, stir, divide between plates and serve as a side dish. Enjoy!

Nutrition: calories 152, fat 3, fiber 3, carbs 5, protein 4

Beet and Garlic

Preparation time: 10 minutes
Cooking time: 18 minutes
Servings: 4

Ingredients:

- 3 beets, washed
- 2 cups water
- 1 tablespoon olive oil
- Salt and black pepper to the taste
- 2 garlic cloves, minced
- 1 teaspoon lemon juice

Directions:

Put the water in your instant pot, add steamer basket, add beets inside, cover, cook on High for 15 minutes, drain, transfer them to a cutting board, cool them down, peel and cut them into medium cubes. Clean your instant pot, set on sauté mode, add oil heat it up, add beets, stir and cook for 3 minutes. Add garlic, lemon juice, salt and pepper, toss well, divide between plates and serve as a side dish, Enjoy!

Nutrition: calories 100, fat 1, fiber 2, carbs 6, protein 3

Green Beans and Tomatoes

Preparation time: 10 minutes
Cooking time: 6 minutes
Servings: 4

Ingredients:

- 2 cups tomatoes, chopped
- 1 tablespoon olive oil
- 1 garlic clove, minced
- 1 pound green beans, trimmed
- Salt to the taste
- ½ tablespoon basil, chopped

Directions:

Set your instant pot on Sauté mode, add oil, heat it up, add garlic, stir and cook for 1 minute. Add tomatoes and green beans, stir, cover and cook on High for 5 minutes. Add salt, pepper and basil, toss well, divide between plates and serve as a side dish. Enjoy!

Nutrition: calories 100, fat 4, fiber 3, carbs 3, protein 2

Bok Choy and Garlic

Preparation time: 10 minutes
Cooking time: 10 minutes
Servings: 4

Ingredients:

- 5 bunches bok choy
- 5 cups water
- 2 garlic cloves, minced
- 1 teaspoon ginger, grated
- 1 tablespoon olive oil
- Salt and black pepper to the taste

Directions:

Put bok choy in your instant pot, add water, cover the pot, cook on High for 7 minutes, drain, chop and transfer to a bowl. Clean your instant pot, set on sauté mode, add oil, heat it up, add bok choy, salt, pepper, garlic and ginger, stir, cook for 2 minutes, divide between plates and serve as a side dish. Enjoy!

Nutrition: calories 100, fat 1, fiber 2, carbs 3, protein 2

Red Cabbage and Applesauce

Preparation time: 10 minutes
Cooking time: 13 minutes
Servings: 4

Ingredients:

- 4 garlic cloves, minced
- ½ cup yellow onion, chopped
- 1 tablespoon olive oil
- 6 cups red cabbage, chopped
- 1 cup water
- 1 tablespoon balsamic vinegar
- 1 cup natural applesauce
- Salt and black pepper to the taste

Directions:

Set your instant pot on Sauté mode, add the oil, heat it up, add onion and garlic, stir and cook for 3 minutes. Add cabbage, water, applesauce, vinegar, salt and pepper, stir, cover, cook on High for 10 minutes, divide between plates and serve as a side dish. Enjoy!

Nutrition: calories 152, fat 4, fiber 6, carbs 10, protein 4

Beets and Capers

Preparation time: 10 minutes
Cooking time: 30 minutes
Servings: 4

Ingredients:
- 4 beets
- 1 cup water
- 2 tablespoons balsamic vinegar
- 2 tablespoons capers
- A bunch of parsley, chopped
- Salt and black pepper to the taste
- 1 tablespoon olive oil
- 1 garlic clove, minced

Directions:

Put the water in your instant pot, add the steamer basket, add beets inside, cover and cook on High for 20 minutes. In a bowl, mix parsley with garlic, salt, pepper, olive oil and capers and whisk. Transfer beets to a cutting board, cool them down, peel and slice them and divide them between plates. Add vinegar and capers mix, toss a bit and serve as a side dish. Enjoy!

Nutrition: calories 63, fat 2, fiber 1, carbs 2, protein 4

Beet and Arugula Side Salad

Preparation time: 10 minutes
Cooking time: 7 minutes
Servings: 4

Ingredients:
- 1 and ½ pounds beets, washed and halved
- 2 teaspoons lemon zest, grated
- 2 tablespoons balsamic vinegar
- 2 tablespoons lemon juice
- 2 tablespoons stevia
- 2 scallions, chopped
- 2 teaspoons mustard
- 2 cups arugula

Directions:

In your instant pot, mix vinegar and lemon juice and beets, stir, cover and cook on High for 7 minutes. Peel beets, roughly chop them and transfer them to a bowl, Add mustard, stevia, scallions and lemon zest and toss. Add arugula, toss well, divide between plates and serve as a side salad. Enjoy!

Nutrition: calories 142, fat 3, fiber 2, carbs 6, protein 4

Tomato and Beet Side Salad

Preparation time: 10 minutes
Cooking time: 30 minutes
Servings: 8

Ingredients:

- 2 and ½ cups water
- 8 small beets, trimmed
- 1 red onion, sliced
- 4 ounces goat cheese
- 1 cup balsamic vinegar
- Salt and black pepper to the taste
- 2 tablespoons stevia
- 1 pint mixed cherry tomatoes, halved
- 2 tablespoons olive oil

Directions:

Put 1 and ½ cups water in your instant pot, add the steamer basket, add beets, cover, cook on High for 20 minutes, transfer them to a cutting board, cool them down, peel, chop and put them into a bowl. Clean your instant pot, add the rest of the water, vinegar, stevia, salt and pepper, stir, set the pot on simmer mode and cook for a couple of minutes. Strain this into a bowl, add onion, leave aside for 10 minutes, drain them well and add to the bowl with the beets. Also add tomatoes, oil, salt, pepper, 2 tablespoons liquid from the onions and goat cheese, toss everything, divide between plates and serve as a side salad. Enjoy!

Nutrition: calories 152, fat 4, fiber 3, carbs 4, protein 3

Broccoli and Garlic

Preparation time: 10 minutes
Cooking time: 12 minutes
Servings: 4

Ingredients:

- 1 broccoli head, cut into 4
- ½ cup water
- 1 tablespoon olive oil
- 6 garlic cloves, minced
- 1 tablespoon balsamic vinegar
- Salt and black pepper to the taste

Directions:

Put the water in your instant pot, add the steamer basket, add broccoli inside, cover, cook on Low for 12 minutes, transfer to a bowl filled with ice water, cool it down and drain it. Clean your instant pot, set it on sauté mode, add oil, heat it up, add garlic, stir and cook for 2 minutes. Add broccoli, vinegar, salt and pepper, stir, cook for 1 minute more, divide among plates and serve as a side dish. Enjoy!

Nutrition: calories 100, fat 2, fiber 1, carbs 2, protein 7

Brussels Sprouts and Dill

Preparation time: 4 minutes
Cooking time: 8 minutes
Servings: 4

Ingredients:

- 1 pound Brussels sprouts, trimmed and halved
- ½ cup bacon, chopped
- Salt and black pepper to the taste
- 1 tablespoon mustard
- 1 cup chicken stock
- 1 tablespoon ghee
- 2 tablespoons dill, chopped

Directions:

Set your instant pot on Sauté mode, add bacon, stir and cook for 2 minutes. Add sprouts, mustard, stock, salt and pepper, stir, cover and cook on High for 4 minutes. Add ghee and dill, stir, set the pot on sauté mode, cook everything for a couple more minutes, divide between plates and serve as a side dish. Enjoy!

Nutrition: calories 162, fat 4, fiber 3, carbs 6, protein 6

Savoy Cabbage and Bacon

Preparation time: 10 minutes
Cooking time: 9 minutes
Servings: 4

Ingredients:

- 1 cup bacon, chopped
- 1 Savoy cabbage head, shredded
- ¼ teaspoon nutmeg, ground
- 1 yellow onion, chopped
- 2 cups beef stock
- Salt and black pepper to the taste
- 1 bay leaf
- 1 cup coconut milk
- 2 tablespoons parsley flakes

Directions:

Set your instant pot on Sauté mode, add bacon and onion, stir and cook for 2 minutes. Add stock, cabbage, bay leaf, salt, pepper and nutmeg, stir, cover, cook on High for 5 minutes, mix with milk and parsley, stir and cook on sauté mode for 4 minutes more. Divide between plates and serve as a side dish. Enjoy!

Nutrition: calories 157, fat 3, fiber 3, carbs 6, protein 6

Sweet Cabbage

Preparation time: 10 minutes
Cooking time: 8 minutes
Servings: 4

Ingredients:
- 1 cabbage, cut into 8 wedges
- 1 tablespoon olive oil
- 1 carrot, grated
- ¼ cup balsamic vinegar
- 1 and ¼ cups water
- 1 teaspoon stevia
- A pinch of cayenne pepper
- ½ teaspoon red pepper flakes

Directions:
Set your instant pot on Sauté mode, add oil, heat it up, add cabbage, stir and cook for 3 minutes. Add carrots, water, stevia, vinegar, cayenne and pepper flakes, stir, cover and cook at High for 5 minutes. Divide between plates and serve right away. Enjoy!

Nutrition: calories 100, fat 3, fiber 3, carbs 4, protein 4

Collard Greens and Tomato Sauce

Preparation time: 10 minutes
Cooking time: 20 minutes
Servings: 4

Ingredients:
- 1 bunch collard greens, trimmed
- 2 tablespoons olive oil
- ½ cup chicken stock
- 2 tablespoons tomato puree
- 1 yellow onion, chopped
- 3 garlic cloves, minced
- Salt and black pepper to the taste
- 1 tablespoon balsamic vinegar
- 1 teaspoon stevia

Directions:
In your instant pot, mix stock with oil, garlic, vinegar, onion, tomato puree, collard greens, salt, pepper and stevia, stir a bit, cover and cook on High for 20 minutes. Divide between plates and serve right away. Enjoy!

Nutrition: calories 132, fat 2, fiber 2, carbs 5, protein 3

Ketogenic Instant Pot Dessert Recipes

Raspberry Dessert

Preparation time: 10 minutes
Cooking time: 2 minutes
Servings: 12

Ingredients:

- ½ cup coconut butter
- ½ cup coconut oil
- ½ cup coconut, unsweetened and shredded
- ½ cup raspberries, dried
- 3 tablespoons stevia

Directions:

Set your instant pot on sauté mode, add coconut butter, melt it, add stevia, oil, coconut and raspberries, stir, cover and cook on High for 2 minutes. Spread this on a lined baking sheet, spread well, introduce in the fridge for a couple of hours, slice and serve. Enjoy!

Nutrition: calories 174, fat 5, fiber 2, carbs 4, protein 7

Blueberries and Strawberries Cream

Preparation time: 10 minutes
Cooking time: 2 minutes
Servings: 12

Ingredients:

- 8 ounces mascarpone cheese
- ¾ teaspoon vanilla stevia
- 1 cup coconut cream
- ½ pint blueberries
- ½ pint strawberries

Directions:

In your instant pot, mix cream with stevia, mascarpone, blueberries and strawberries, stir, cover and cook on High for 2 minutes. Divide into small dessert bowls and serve cold. Enjoy!

Nutrition: calories 183, fat 4, fiber 1, carbs 3, protein 1

Lemon Cream

Preparation time: 10 minutes
Cooking time: 2 minutes
Servings: 5

Ingredients:

- 1 cup coconut cream
- A pinch of salt
- 1 teaspoon lemon stevia
- ¼ cup lemon juice
- 8 ounces mascarpone cheese

Directions:

In your instant pot, mix cream with mascarpone, lemon juice, stevia and a pinch of salt, stir, cover and cook on High for 2 minutes. Divide into small dessert bowls and keep in the fridge until you serve it. Enjoy!

Nutrition: calories 165, fat 7, fiber 0, carbs 2, protein 3

Cream Cheese Bars

Preparation time: 10 minutes
Cooking time: 16 minutes
Servings: 8

Ingredients:

- 5 ounces coconut oil, melted
- ½ teaspoon baking powder
- 4 tablespoons stevia
- 1 teaspoon vanilla extract
- 4 ounces cream cheese
- 6 eggs
- ½ cup blueberries
- 1 and ½ cups water

Directions:

In a bowl, mix oil with eggs, cream cheese, vanilla, stevia, blueberries and baking powder, blend using an immersion blender and pour into a baking dish. Add the water to your instant pot, add steamer basket, add baking dish inside, cover and cook on High for 16 minutes. Leave aside to cool down, cut into medium bars and serve them cold. Enjoy!

Nutrition: calories 162, fat 4, fiber 2, carbs 6, protein 8

Cocoa Pudding

Preparation time: 50 minutes
Cooking time: 3 minutes
Servings: 2

Ingredients:

- 1 and ½ cups water+ 2 tablespoons water
- 1 tablespoon gelatin
- 2 tablespoons stevia
- 2 tablespoons cocoa powder
- 1 cup coconut milk, hot

Directions:

In a bowl, mix milk with stevia and cocoa powder and stir well. In a bowl, mix gelatin with 2 tablespoons water, stir well, add to the cocoa mix, stir and divide into 2 ramekins. Add the water to your instant pot, add the steamer basket, add ramekins inside, cover and cook on High for 3 minutes. Keep puddings in the fridge until you serve. Enjoy!

Nutrition: calories 120, fat 2, fiber 1, carbs 4, protein 3

Avocado Pudding

Preparation time: 10 minutes
Cooking time: 2 minutes
Servings: 4

Ingredients:

- 2 avocados, pitted, peeled and chopped
- 2 teaspoons vanilla extract
- 80 drops stevia
- 1 tablespoon lime juice
- 14 ounces coconut milk
- 1 and ½ cups water

Directions:

In your instant pot, mix avocado with coconut milk, vanilla extract, stevia and lime juice, blend well and divide into 4 ramekins. Add the water to your instant pot, add the steamer basket, add ramekins inside, cover and cook on High for 2 minutes. Keep puddings in the fridge until you serve them. Enjoy!

Nutrition: calories 150, fat 3, fiber 1, carbs 3, protein 4

Peppermint Pudding

Preparation time: 2 hours
Cooking time: 2 minutes
Servings: 3

Ingredients:

- ½ cup coconut oil, melted
- 13 stevia drops
- 1 tablespoon cocoa powder
- 1 teaspoon peppermint oil
- 14 ounces canned coconut milk
- 1 avocado, pitted, peeled and chopped
- 10 drops stevia

Directions:

In a bowl, mix coconut oil with cocoa powder and 3 drops stevia, stir well, transfer to a lined container, keep in the fridge for 1 hour and chop into small pieces. In your instant pot, mix coconut milk with avocado, 10 drops stevia and peppermint oil, blend using an immersion blender, cover pot and cook on High for 2 minutes. Add chocolate chips, stir, divide pudding into bowls and keep in the fridge for 1 hour before serving. Enjoy!

Nutrition: calories 140, fat 3, fiber 2, carbs 3, protein 4

Coconut Pudding

Preparation time: 10 minutes
Cooking time: 3 minutes
Servings: 4

Ingredients:

- 1 and 2/3 cups coconut milk
- 1 tablespoon gelatin
- 6 tablespoons swerve
- 3 egg yolks
- ½ teaspoon vanilla extract

Directions:

In a bowl, mix gelatin with 1 tablespoon coconut milk, stir well and leave aside for now. Set your instant pot on simmer mode, add milk, heat it up, add swerve, egg yolks, vanilla extract and gelatin, stir well, cover pot and cook on High for 2 minutes. Divide everything into 4 ramekins and serve them cold. Enjoy!

Nutrition: calories 140, fat 2, fiber 1, carbs 3, protein 2

Orange Cake

Preparation time: 10 minutes
Cooking time: 25 minutes
Servings: 12

Ingredients:

- 6 eggs
- 1 orange, cut into quarters
- 1 and ½ cups water
- 1 teaspoon vanilla extract
- 1 teaspoon baking powder
- 9 ounces almond meal
- 4 tablespoons swerve
- 2 tablespoons orange zest, grated
- 2 ounces stevia
- 4 ounces cream cheese
- 4 ounces coconut yogurt

Directions:

In your food processor, mix orange with almond meal, swerve, eggs, baking powder and vanilla extract, pulse well and transfer to a cake pan. Add the water to your instant pot, add steamer basket, add cake pan inside, cover and cook on High for 25 minutes. In a bowl, mix cream cheese with orange zest, coconut yogurt and stevia and stir well. Spread this well over cake, slice and serve it. Enjoy!

Nutrition: calories 170, fat 13, fiber 2, carbs 4, protein 4

Walnuts Cream

Preparation time: 10 minutes
Cooking time: 1 minute
Servings: 6

Ingredients:

- 2 ounces coconut oil
- 4 tablespoons cocoa powder
- 1 teaspoon vanilla extract
- 1 cup walnuts, chopped
- 4 tablespoons stevia

Directions:

In your instant pot, mix cocoa powder with oil, vanilla, walnuts and stevia, blend using an immersion blender, cover pot and cook on High for 1 minute. Transfer to a bowl, leave in the fridge for a couple of hours and serve. Enjoy!

Nutrition: calories 100, fat 5, fiber 1, carbs 3, protein 4

Lemon Cream

Preparation time: 10 minutes
Cooking time: 30 minutes
Servings: 6

Ingredients:
- 1 and 1/3 pint coconut milk
- 1 and ½ cups water
- 4 tablespoons lemon zest
- 4 eggs
- 5 tablespoons swerve
- 2 tablespoons lemon juice

Directions:

In a bowl, mix eggs with milk, swerve, lemon zest and lemon juice, whisk well and pour into 6 ramekins. Add the water to your instant pot, add steamer basket, add ramekins, cover pot and cook on High for 20 minutes. Leave cream to cool down before servings. Enjoy!

Nutrition: calories 120, fat 2, fiber 2, carbs 5, protein 3

Chocolate Cream

Preparation time: 1 minute
Cooking time: 3 minutes
Servings: 6

Ingredients:
- ½ cup coconut cream
- 4 ounces dark chocolate, unsweetened and chopped

Directions:

In your instant pot, mix cream with dark chocolate, cover pot and cook on High for 3 minutes. Stir your cream really well, divide into dessert cups and serve cold. Enjoy!

Nutrition: calories 78, fat 2, fiber 1, carbs 3, protein 1

Berry Cream

Preparation time: 10 minutes
Cooking time: 2 minutes
Servings: 4

Ingredients:
- 3 tablespoons cocoa powder
- 14 ounces coconut cream
- 1 cup blackberries
- 1 cup raspberries
- 2 tablespoons stevia

Directions:
In your instant pot, mix cream with cocoa, stevia, blackberries and raspberries, stir, cover and cook on High for 2 minutes. Divide into dessert cups and serve cold. Enjoy!

Nutrition: calories 145, fat 4, fiber 2, carbs 6, protein 2

Strawberry Cream

Preparation time: 10 minutes
Cooking time: 2 minutes
Servings: 4

Ingredients:
- 1 and ¾ cups coconut cream
- 2 teaspoons stevia
- 1 cup strawberries

Directions:
In your instant pot, mix cream with stevia and strawberries, stir, cover and cook on High for 2 minutes. Divide into bowls and serve cold. Enjoy!

Nutrition: calories 155, fat 2, fiber 1, carbs 5, protein 4

Caramel Pudding

Preparation time: 10 minutes
Cooking time: 25 minutes
Servings: 2

Ingredients:

- 1 and ½ teaspoons caramel extract
- 1 cup water
- 2 ounces cream cheese

- 2 eggs
- 1 and ½ tablespoons swerve

For the sauce:

- 2 tablespoons swerve
- 2 tablespoons ghee

- ¼ teaspoon caramel extract

Directions:

In your blender, mix cream cheese with water, 1 and ½ tablespoons swerve, 1 and ½ teaspoons caramel extract and eggs, pulse well and divide into 2 greased ramekins. Add the water to your instant pot, add steamer basket, add ramekins inside, cover and cook on High for 20 minutes. Meanwhile, put the ghee in a pot, heat up over medium heat, add ¼ teaspoon caramel extract and 2 tablespoons swerve, stir well, cook for a few minutes and pour over caramel pudding. Enjoy!

Nutrition: calories 174, fat 7, fiber 1, carbs 2, protein 4

Peanut and Chia Pudding

Preparation time: 10 minutes
Cooking time: 2 minutes
Servings: 4

Ingredients:

- ½ cup chia seeds
- 2 cups almond milk, unsweetened
- 1 teaspoon vanilla extract

- ¼ cup peanut butter, unsweetened
- 1 teaspoon vanilla stevia

Directions:

In your instant pot, mix milk with chia seeds, peanut butter, vanilla extract and stevia, stir, cover and cook on High for 2 minutes. Divide into dessert glasses and leave in the fridge for 10 minutes before serving, Enjoy!

Nutrition: calories 120, fat 1, fiber 2, carbs 4, protein 2

Pumpkin Cream

Preparation time: 10 minutes
Cooking time: 5 minutes
Servings: 6

Ingredients:

- 1 tablespoon gelatin
- ¼ cup warm water
- 14 ounces coconut milk
- 14 ounces pumpkin puree
- A pinch of salt
- 2 teaspoons vanilla extract
- 1 teaspoon cinnamon powder
- 1 teaspoon pumpkin pie spice
- 8 scoops stevia
- 3 tablespoons erythritol

Directions:

In your instant pot, mix pumpkin puree with coconut milk, a pinch of salt, vanilla extract, cinnamon powder, stevia, erythritol and pumpkin pie spice, stir well, cover and cook on High for 4 minutes. In a bowl, mix gelatin and water and stir. Add this over pumpkin cream, stir, divide custard into ramekins and serve them cold. Enjoy!

Nutrition: calories 160, fat 2, fiber 1, carbs 3, protein 4

Chia Jam

Preparation time: 15 minutes
Cooking time: 5 minutes
Servings: 22

Ingredients:

- 3 tablespoons chia seeds
- 2 and ½ cups cherries, pitted
- ½ teaspoon vanilla powder
- Zest from ½ lemon, grated
- ¼ cup erythritol
- 10 drops stevia
- 1 cup water

Directions:

In your instant pot, mix cherries with water, stevia, erythritol, vanilla powder, chia seeds and lemon peel, stir, cover and cook on High for 5 minutes. Divide into dessert cups and serve cold. Enjoy!

Nutrition: calories 160, fat 1, fiber 1, carbs 2, protein 0.5

Melon Cream

Preparation time: 5 minutes
Cooking time: 10 minutes
Servings: 6

Ingredients:

- Flesh from 1 melon
- 1 ounce stevia
- 1 cup natural apple juice
- 1 tablespoon ghee
- Juice of 1 lemon

Directions:

Put melon and apple juice in your instant pot, cover, cook on High for 7 minutes, transfer to a blender, add lemon juice, ghee and stevia, pulse well and return to your instant pot. Set on simmer mode, cook for a couple more minutes, divide into dessert cups and serve. Enjoy!

Nutrition: calories 73, fat 1, fiber 1, carbs 2, protein 2

Peach Cream

Preparation time: 5 minutes
Cooking time: 3 minutes
Servings: 6

Ingredients:

- 10 ounces peaches, stoned and chopped
- A pinch of nutmeg, ground
- 2 tablespoons coconut flakes
- 3 tablespoons stevia
- ½ cup water
- 1/8 teaspoon cinnamon powder
- 1/8 teaspoon almond extract

Directions:

In your instant pot, mix peaches with nutmeg, coconut, stevia, almond extract and cinnamon, stir, cover and cook at High for 3 minutes. Divide into small cups and serve. Enjoy!

Nutrition: calories 90, fat 2, fiber 1, carbs 3, protein 5

Peaches and Sweet Sauce

Preparation time: 10 minutes
Cooking time: 10 minutes
Servings: 6

Ingredients:
- 4 tablespoons stevia
- 3 cups peaches, cored and roughly chopped
- 6 tablespoons natural apple juice
- 2 teaspoons lemon zest, grated

Directions:

In your instant pot mix peaches with stevia, apple juice and lemon zest, stir, cover and cook at High for 10 minutes. Divide into small cups and serve cold. Enjoy!

Nutrition: calories 80, fat 2, fiber 2, carbs 5, protein 5

Chestnut Cream

Preparation time: 10 minutes
Cooking time: 20 minutes
Servings: 6

Ingredients:
- 11 ounces stevia
- 11 ounces water
- 1 and ½ pounds chestnuts, halved and peeled

Directions:

In your instant pot, mix stevia with water and chestnuts, stir, cover and cook on High for 20 minutes. Blend using your immersion blender, divide into small cups and serve. Enjoy!

Nutrition: calories 82, fat 1, fiber 0, carbs 5, protein 3

Cheesecake

Preparation time: 60 minutes
Cooking time: 50 minutes
Servings: 12

Ingredients:

For the crust:
- 4 tablespoons melted ghee
- 1 and ½ cups chocolate cookie crumbs

For the filling:
- 24 ounces cream cheese, soft
- 2 tablespoons coconut flakes
- 3 tablespoons stevia
- 3 eggs
- 1 tablespoon vanilla extract
- Cooking spray
- 1 cup water
- ½ cup Greek yogurt
- 5 ounces white chocolate, unsweetened and melted
- 5 ounces bittersweet chocolate, melted

Directions:

In a bowl mix cookie crumbs with ghee, stir well, press on the bottom of a cake pan that you've greased with cooking spray, and lined with parchment paper. In a bowl, mix cream cheese with coconut, stevia, eggs, vanilla and yogurt, whisk well and leave aside for a few minutes. Put milk chocolate in a heatproof bowl and heat up in the microwave for 30 seconds. Add white and bittersweet chocolate, stir well again and pour over cookie crust. Add the water to your instant pot, add steamer basket, and cake, cover and cook on High for 45 minutes. Slice and serve cold. Enjoy!

Nutrition: calories 267, fat 4, fiber 7, carbs 10, protein 7

Banana Cake

Preparation time: 10 minutes
Cooking time: 30 minutes
Servings: 6

Ingredients:
- 4 tablespoons stevia
- 1/3 cup ghee, soft
- 1 teaspoon vanilla extract
- 1 egg
- 2 bananas, peeled and mashed
- 1 teaspoon baking powder
- 1 and ½ cups coconut flour
- ½ teaspoons baking soda
- 1/3 cup coconut milk
- 1 and ½ teaspoons keto cream of tartar
- 2 cups water
- Olive oil cooking spray

Directions:

In a bowl, mix milk with cream of tartar, stevia, ghee, egg, vanilla and bananas and stir everything. Add flour, baking powder and baking soda, stir well and pour into a cake pan that you've greased with cooking spray. Add the water to your instant pot, add steamer basket, and cake pan, cover and cook on High for 30 minutes. Slice and serve cold. Enjoy!

Nutrition: calories 214, fat 2, fiber 2, carbs 6, protein 8

Pumpkin Cake

Preparation time: 10 minutes
Cooking time: 35 minutes
Servings: 12

Ingredients:

- 2 cups coconut flour
- 1 teaspoon baking soda
- ¾ teaspoon pumpkin pie spice
- ¾ cup stevia
- 1 banana, mashed
- ½ teaspoon baking powder
- 2 tablespoons coconut oil
- ½ cup Greek yogurt
- 8 ounces canned pumpkin puree
- Cooking spray
- 1-quart water
- 1 egg
- ½ teaspoon vanilla extract
- 2/3 cup chocolate chips

Directions:

In a bowl, mix flour with baking soda, baking powder, pumpkin spice, stevia, oil, banana, yogurt, pumpkin puree, vanilla and egg and stir using a mixer. Add chocolate chips, stir, pour into a cake pan greased with cooking spray and cover with some tin foil. Add the water to your instant pot, add steamer basket, add cake pan inside, cover and cook on High for 35 minutes. Slice cake and serve cold. Enjoy!

Nutrition: calories 200, fat 3, fiber 3, carbs 6, protein 8

Apple Cake

Preparation time: 10 minutes
Cooking time: 1 hour and 10 minutes
Servings: 6

Ingredients:

- 3 cups apples, cored and cubed
- 4 tablespoons stevia
- 1 tablespoon vanilla extract
- 2 eggs
- 1 tablespoon apple pie spice
- 2 cups coconut flour
- 2 tablespoons ghee, melted
- 1 tablespoon baking powder
- 1 cup water

Directions:

In a bowl mix egg with ghee, apple pie spice, stevia, apples, flour and baking powder, stir and pour into a cake pan. Add the water to your instant pot, add steamer basket, add cake pan inside, cover and cook on High for 1 hour. Leave the cake to cool down, slice and serve. Enjoy!

Nutrition: calories 89, fat 1, fiber 2, carbs 5, protein 4

Upside Down Cake

Preparation time: 10 minutes
Cooking time: 25 minutes
Servings: 8

Ingredients:

- 1 apple, sliced
- 1 apple, chopped
- 1 cup ricotta cheese
- 3 tablespoons stevia
- 1 tablespoon lemon juice
- 1 egg
- 1 teaspoon vanilla extract
- 3 tablespoons olive oil
- 1 cup coconut flour
- 2 teaspoons baking powder
- 1/8 teaspoon cinnamon powder
- 1 teaspoon baking soda
- 2 cups water

Directions:

In a bowl, mix all apples with lemon juice and half of the stevia, toss and leave aside. Line a cake pan with some parchment paper, grease with some oil, dust with some flour and spread half of the apples. In a bowl, mix the egg with cheese, the rest of the stevia, vanilla extract, oil, flour, baking powder and soda, the rest of the apples and cinnamon and stir. Pour everything into the cake pan and cover with tin foil. Add the water to your instant pot, add steamer basket, and cake pan, cover and cook on High for 25 minutes. Turn cake upside down, slice and serve. Enjoy!

Nutrition: calories 210, fat 4, fiber 5, carbs 12, protein 5

Almond Cake

Preparation time: 10 minutes
Cooking time: 20 minutes
Servings: 4

Ingredients:

- 1/8 teaspoon almond extract
- 2 cups water
- 1 cup coconut flour
- ½ cup cocoa powder
- 4 tablespoons stevia
- 3 tablespoons olive oil
- 3 eggs
- 2 teaspoons baking powder
- ½ cup almonds, sliced

Directions:

In a bowl, mix cocoa powder, almond extract, flour, eggs, stevia, oil, baking powder and almonds, whisk well and pour everything into a greased cake pan. Add the water to your instant pot, add steamer basket, and cake pan, cover and cook on High for 20 minutes. Slice and serve cold. Enjoy!

Nutrition: calories 162, fat 4, fiber 2, carbs 18, protein 3

French Coconut Cream

Preparation time: 1 hour
Cooking time: 15 minutes
Servings: 6

Ingredients:
- 2 cups coconut cream
- 1 teaspoon cinnamon powder
- 6 egg yolks
- 5 tablespoons stevia
- Zest from 1 lemon, grated
- A pinch of nutmeg
- 2 cups water

Directions:
Heat up a pan with the coconut cream over medium heat, add cinnamon and orange zest, stir, bring to a simmer, take off heat and leave aside to cool down. Add egg yolks and stevia, stir well, strain and divide this into small ramekins. Add the water to your instant pot, add steamer basket, add ramekins, cover pot and cook on Low for 10 minutes. Sprinkle nutmeg on top and serve cold. Enjoy!

Nutrition: calories 200, fat 5, fiber 2, carbs 10, protein 13

Flavored Pears

Preparation time: 10 minutes
Cooking time: 10 minutes
Servings: 4

Ingredients:
- 4 pears
- Juice of 1 lemon
- Zest from 1 lemon, grated
- 26 ounces grape juice
- ½ vanilla bean
- 4 peppercorns
- 2 rosemary sprigs

Directions:
In your instant pot, mix grape juice with lemon juice, lemon zest, vanilla, rosemary, peppercorns and pears, cover pot and cook on High for 10 minutes. Divide into bowls and serve. Enjoy!

Nutrition: calories 152, fat 3, fiber 6, carbs 8, protein 12

Pumpkin Pudding

Preparation time: 30 minutes
Cooking time: 18 minutes
Servings: 6

Ingredients:

- 1 cup cauliflower rice
- ½ cup water
- 3 cups coconut milk
- ½ cup dates, chopped
- 1 cinnamon stick
- 1 cup pumpkin puree
- 4 tablespoons stevia
- 1 teaspoon vanilla extract

Directions:

Put cauliflower rice in your instant pot, add water, milk, dates and cinnamon, stir, cover and cook on High for 13 minutes. Add pumpkin puree, stevia and vanilla, stir, set the pot on Simmer mode and cook for 5 minutes. Discard cinnamon, divide pudding into bowls and serve. Enjoy!

Nutrition: calories 120, fat 3, fiber 3, carbs 8, protein 5

Strawberries and Cranberries Marmalade

Preparation time: 10 minutes
Cooking time: 15 minutes
Servings: 8

Ingredients:

- 1 pound cranberries
- 1 pound strawberries
- ½ pound blueberries
- 3.5 ounces blackcurrant
- Stevia to the taste
- Zest from 1 lemon, grated
- ½ cup water

Directions:

In your instant pot, mix strawberries with cranberries, blueberries, currants, lemon zest, stevia and water, stir, set the pot on simmer mode, cook for 5 minutes, then cover and cook on High for 10 minutes. Divide into dessert cups and serve. Enjoy!

Nutrition: calories 100, fat 0, fiber 1, carbs 7, protein 3

Pear Marmalade

Preparation time: 10 minutes
Cooking time: 4 minutes
Servings: 12

Ingredients:
- 8 pears, cored and roughly chopped
- 2 apples, peeled, cored and roughly chopped
- ¼ cup natural apple juice
- 1 teaspoon cinnamon powder

Directions:

In your instant pot, mix pears with apples, cinnamon and apple juice, stir, cover, cook on High for 4 minutes, blend with your immersion blender, leave aside to cool down, divide into small dessert cups and serve. Enjoy!

Nutrition: calories 90, fat 0, fiber 2, carbs 19, protein 2

Peach Marmalade

Preparation time: 10 minutes
Cooking time: 10 minutes
Servings: 6

Ingredients:
- 4 and ½ cups peaches, peeled and cubed
- Stevia to the taste
- 1 teaspoon ginger, grated
- 2 cups water

Directions:

In your instant pot, mix peaches with stevia, ginger and water, stir, cover and cook on High for 10 minutes. Divide into small cups, cool down and serve. Enjoy!

Nutrition: calories 82, fat 1, fiber 2, carbs 3, protein 2

Strawberries Compote

Preparation time: 10 minutes
Cooking time: 7 minutes
Servings: 8

Ingredients:

- 1 cup blueberries
- 2 cups strawberries, chopped
- 2 tablespoons lemon juice
- Stevia to the taste
- 1 tablespoon water

Directions:

In your instant pot, mix blueberries with strawberries, lemon juice, stevia and water, stir, cover and cook on High for 7 minutes. Divide into cups and serve cold. Enjoy!

Nutrition: calories 200, fat 1, fiber 3, carbs 12, protein 3

Sweet Peaches

Preparation time: 10 minutes
Cooking time: 6 minutes
Servings: 3

Ingredients:

- 6 peaches, insides discarded
- ¼ cup coconut flour
- 2 tablespoons stevia
- 2 tablespoons coconut butter
- ½ teaspoon cinnamon powder
- 1 teaspoon almond extract
- 1 cup water

Directions:

In a bowl, mix flour with stevia, butter, cinnamon and almond, stir well and stuff peaches with this mix. Add the water to your instant pot, add steamer basket, add peaches, cover and cook on High for 6 minutes. Divide into cups and serve them cold. Enjoy!

Nutrition: calories 152, fat 2, fiber 2, carbs 9, protein 3

Simple Peach Compote

Preparation time: 10 minutes
Cooking time: 4 minutes
Servings: 4

Ingredients:

- 8 peaches, chopped
- Stevia to the taste
- 1 teaspoon cinnamon powder
- 1 teaspoon vanilla extract
- 1 cup water

Directions:

In your instant pot, mix peaches with stevia, water, cinnamon and vanilla, stir, cover and cook on High for 4 minutes. Divide into bowls and serve cold. Enjoy!

Nutrition: calories 120, fat 2, fiber 2, carbs 8, protein 2

Apple Cobbler

Preparation time: 10 minutes
Cooking time: 12 minutes
Servings: 4

Ingredients:

- 3 apples, cored and roughly chopped
- 2 pears, cored and roughly chopped
- 1 and ½ cup hot water
- 2 tablespoons coconut flakes
- 3 tablespoon stevia
- 1 teaspoon cinnamon powder

Directions:

In your instant pot, mix apples with pears, water, coconut, stevia and cinnamon, stir, cover and cook on High for 12 minutes. Divide into bowls and serve cold. Enjoy!

Nutrition: calories 162, fat 2, fiber 2, carbs 6, protein 2

Zucchini Cake

Preparation time: 10 minutes
Cooking time: 25 minutes
Servings: 6

Ingredients:

- 1 cup natural applesauce
- 3 eggs, whisked
- 1 tablespoon vanilla extract
- 4 tablespoons stevia
- 2 cups zucchini, grated
- 2 and ½ cups coconut flour
- ½ cup baking cocoa powder
- 1 teaspoon baking soda
- ¼ teaspoon baking powder
- 1 teaspoon cinnamon powder
- ½ cup walnuts, chopped
- 2 cups water

Directions:

In a bowl, mix zucchini with stevia, vanilla, eggs, applesauce, flour, cocoa powder, baking soda, baking powder, cinnamon and walnuts, stir and pour into a cake pan. Add the water to your instant pot, add steamer basket, and cake pan, cover and cook on High for 20 minutes. Slice and serve cold. Enjoy!

Nutrition: calories 192, fat 3, fiber 6, carbs 8, protein 3

Pineapple and Cauliflower Pudding

Preparation time: 10 minutes
Cooking time: 5 minutes
Servings: 8

Ingredients:

- 1 tablespoon coconut oil
- 1 and ½ cups water
- 1 cup cauliflower rice
- 14 ounces coconut milk
- 8 ounces pineapple, chopped
- 2 eggs, whisked
- 4 tablespoons stevia
- ½ teaspoon vanilla extract

Directions:

In your instant pot, mix oil, water and cauliflower rice, stir, cover, cook on High for 3 minutes and mix with coconut milk and stevia. Add eggs, vanilla and pineapple, stir, cover again and cook on High for 2 minutes more. Divide into bowls and serve cold. Enjoy!

Nutrition: calories 100, fat 4, fiber 1, carbs 6, protein 4

Chocolate Pudding

Preparation time: 10 minutes
Cooking time: 20 minutes
Servings: 4

Ingredients:

- 6 ounces dark chocolate, chopped and melted
- ½ cup hot coconut milk
- 1 cup coconut cream
- 5 egg yolks
- 4 tablespoons stevia
- 2 teaspoons vanilla extract
- 2 cups water
- ¼ teaspoon cardamom powder

Directions:

In a bowl, mix egg yolks with vanilla, stevia, cardamom, melted chocolate, coconut milk and coconut cream, whisk really well and strain into 4 ramekins. Add the water to your instant pot, add steamer basket, add ramekins inside, cover and cook on High for 12 minutes. Serve cold. Enjoy!

Nutrition: calories 162, fat 4, fiber 1, carbs 12, protein 7

Strawberries Compote

Preparation time: 10 minutes
Cooking time: 30 minutes
Servings: 4

Ingredients:

- 1/3 cup water
- 1 pound strawberries, chopped
- 1 pound rhubarb, chopped
- 3 tablespoon stevia
- 1 tablespoon mint, chopped
- 1 pound strawberries, chopped

Directions:

In your instant pot, mix water with strawberries, rhubarb and stevia, stir, cover and cook on High for 20 minutes. Add mint, stir, divide into cups and serve cold. Enjoy!

Nutrition: calories 91, fat 1, fiber 1, carbs 8, protein 1

Carrot, Pecans and Raisins Cake

Preparation time: 10 minutes
Cooking time: 1 hour
Servings: 6

Ingredients:

- 1 and ½ cups water
- A drizzle of coconut oil, melted
- 4 tablespoons stevia
- 2 eggs
- ½ cup coconut flour
- ½ teaspoon allspice
- ½ teaspoon cinnamon powder
- A pinch of nutmeg
- ½ teaspoon baking soda
- ½ cup pecans, chopped
- ½ cup carrots, grated
- ½ cup raisins
- 1 cup coconut flakes

For the sauce:

- 4 tablespoons ghee
- Stevia to the taste
- ¼ cup coconut cream
- ¼ teaspoon cinnamon powder

Directions:

In a bowl, mix eggs with 4 tablespoons stevia, flour, allspice, cinnamon powder, nutmeg, baking soda, carrots, pecans, raisins and coconut flakes, whisk well and pour into a cake pan greased with some coconut oil. Add the water to your instant pot, add the steamer basket, add cake pan inside, cover and cook on High for 50 minutes. Meanwhile, heat up a pan with the ghee over medium heat, add stevia to the taste, coconut cream and cinnamon powder, stir and cook for 2 minutes. Drizzle this over cake, slice and serve. Enjoy!

Nutrition: calories 271, fat 4, fiber 4, carbs 17, protein 6

Fresh Figs

Preparation time: 10 minutes
Cooking time: 3 minutes
Servings: 4

Ingredients:

- 1 cup natural grape juice
- 1 pound figs
- ½ cup pine nuts, toasted
- 4 tablespoons stevia

Directions:

In your instant pot, mix grape juice with figs and stevia, cover pot and cook on High for 3 minutes. Divide this into bowls, sprinkle pine nuts on top and serve. Enjoy!

Nutrition: calories 100, fat 0, fiber 1, carbs 9, protein 1

Sweet Carrots

Preparation time: 10 minutes
Cooking time: 10 minutes
Servings: 4

Ingredients:
- 1 tablespoon stevia
- 2 cups baby carrots
- 1 tablespoon ghee
- ½ cup water

Directions:

In your instant pot, mix carrots with stevia, ghee and water, stir, cover and cook on High for 10 minutes. Divide into dessert cups and serve. Enjoy!

Nutrition: calories 100, fat 1, fiber 1, carbs 2, protein 2

Pear Pudding

Preparation time: 5 minutes
Cooking time: 7 minutes
Servings: 4

Ingredients:
- 1 cup water
- 2 cups pears, chopped
- 2 cups coconut milk
- 1 tablespoon ghee
- 3 tablespoons stevia
- ½ teaspoon cinnamon powder
- 1 cup coconut flakes
- ½ cup walnuts, chopped

Directions:

In a pudding pan, mix milk with stevia, ghee, coconut, cinnamon, pears and walnuts and stir. Add the water to your instant pot, add steamer basket, add pudding pan, cover and cook on High for 7 minutes. Divide into bowls and serve. Enjoy!

Nutrition: calories 172, fat 3, fiber 4, carbs 8, protein 7

Winter Fruit Cobbler

Preparation time: 10 minutes
Cooking time: 10 minutes
Servings: 4

Ingredients:

- 1 plum, chopped
- 1 and ½ cups water
- 1 pear, chopped
- 1 apple, chopped
- 2 tablespoons stevia
- 3 tablespoons coconut oil
- ½ teaspoon cinnamon powder
- ¼ cup pecans, toasted and chopped
- ¼ cup coconut, shredded

Directions:

In a bowl, mix plum with pear, apple, stevia, oil, cinnamon, coconut and pecans, stir and transfer to a round pan. Add water to your instant pot, add steamer basket, add pan inside, cover and cook on High for 10 minutes. Divide into bowls and serve. Enjoy!

Nutrition: calories 152, fat 2, fiber 2, carbs 8, protein 7

Pumpkin Granola

Preparation time: 10 minutes
Cooking time: 13 minutes
Servings: 6

Ingredients:

- 2 cups water
- 1 tablespoon melted ghee
- 1 cup pumpkin puree
- 1 cup coconut flakes
- 3 tablespoons stevia
- 2 teaspoons cinnamon powder
- 1 teaspoon pumpkin pie spice

Directions:

Set your instant pot on sauté mode, add ghee, heat it up, add coconut flakes, pumpkin, water, cinnamon, stevia and spice, stir, cover and cook on High for 13 minutes. Divide into bowls and serve. Enjoy!

Nutrition: calories 182, fat 2, fiber 1, carbs 8, protein 4

Carrot and Chia Seed Pudding

Preparation time: 10 minutes
Cooking time: 10 minutes
Servings: 4

Ingredients:

- 1 cup coconut flakes
- 2 cups water
- 1 tablespoon ghee
- 3 tablespoons stevia
- 2 teaspoons cinnamon powder
- 1 cup carrots, grated
- ¼ cup chia seeds

Directions:

Select the Sauté mode on your instant pot, add ghee, heat it up, add coconut, water, stevia, cinnamon, carrots and chia seeds, stir, cover and cook on High for 10 minutes. Divide into bowls and serve cold. Enjoy!

Nutrition: calories 132, fat 2, fiber 2, carbs 9, protein 4

Cinnamon Rice Pudding

Preparation time: 10 minutes
Cooking time: 10 minutes
Servings: 4

Ingredients:

- 1 and ½ cups cauliflower rice
- 1 and ½ teaspoon cinnamon powder
- 4 tablespoons stevia
- 2 tablespoons ghee
- 2 apples, cored and sliced
- 1 cup natural apple juice
- 3 cups coconut milk

Directions:

Set your instant pot on Sauté mode, add ghee, heat it up, add cauliflower rice, stevia, apples, apple juice, milk and cinnamon, stir, cover and cook on High for 10 minutes. Divide into bowls and serve warm. Enjoy!

Nutrition: calories 110, fat 2, fiber 3, carbs 12, protein 4

Ketogenic Instant Pot Breakfast Recipes

Colored Cauliflower and Eggs Breakfast

Preparation time: 10 minutes
Cooking time: 15 minutes
Servings: 2

Ingredients:

- 1 cauliflower head, florets separated and chopped
- 1 tablespoon olive oil
- 1 small yellow onion, chopped
- ¼ red bell pepper, sliced
- ¼ yellow bell pepper, sliced
- ¼ green bell pepper, sliced
- ¼ teaspoon poultry seasoning
- ¼ teaspoon dill, dried
- A pinch of salt and black pepper
- 2 eggs
- 1 cup water+ 2 tablespoons

Directions:

Put the cauliflower in a heatproof bowl, add some water, introduce in your microwave for a couple of minutes, drain and leave aside for now. Set your instant pot on sauté mode, add the oil, heat it up, add onion, red, green and yellow bell pepper, stir and cook for 2-3 minutes. Add cauliflower and 2 tablespoons water, stir and cook for 2 minutes more. Add dill, salt, pepper, and poultry seasoning, stir cook for 2 minutes more, transfer to a heatproof dish and crack eggs on top. Clean your instant pot, add 1 cup water and the trivet, add dish inside, cover and cook on High for 6 minutes. Divide between 2 plates and serve for breakfast. Enjoy!

Nutrition: calories 200, fat 3, fiber 4, carbs 7, protein 4

Simple Breakfast Hash Browns

Preparation time: 10 minutes
Cooking time: 10 minutes
Servings: 2

Ingredients:

- 1 egg, whisked
- A pinch of salt and black pepper
- 2 cups cauliflower, riced
- 1 teaspoon red bell pepper, chopped
- 1tablespoon onion, chopped
- 1 teaspoon green bell pepper, chopped
- ½ tablespoon olive oil
- 1 cup water
- 1 small block onion and chives cheese, grated

Directions:

Set your instant pot on sauté mode, add the oil heat it up, add onion, stir and cook for 2 minutes. Add cauliflower rice, red and green bell pepper, stir, cook for 1 minute more and transfer everything to a bowl. Cool this down, add salt, pepper and egg and whisk everything. Pour this into a greased baking dish and sprinkle onion and chives cheese all over. Clean your instant pot, add the water, and the trivet, and the dish with the cauliflower mix inside, cover pot and cook on High for 6 minutes. Divide between 2 plates and serve for breakfast. Enjoy!

Nutrition: calories 100, fat 4, fiber 2, carbs 8, protein 5

Delicious Breakfast Meatloaf

Preparation time: 10 minutes
Cooking time: 20 minutes
Servings: 4

Ingredients:
- 1 pound Italian sausage
- 4 ounces cream cheese
- 6 eggs
- 1 tablespoon ghee
- 2 cups water
- 1 small yellow onion, chopped
- 2 tablespoons scallions, chopped
- 1 cup cheddar cheese, shredded

Directions:

In a bowl, mix sausage with half of the cheese, eggs, onion and scallions and stir really well. Grease a loaf pan with the ghee, add sausage mixture and spread evenly. Add the rest of the cream cheese and sprinkle cheddar cheese on top. Add the water to your instant pot, add the steamer basket, add loaf pan inside, cover pot and cook on High for 15 minutes. Take loaf pan out of the instant pot, introduce in preheated broiler and broil for 5 minutes. Slice, divide between plates and serve for breakfast. Enjoy!

Nutrition: calories 200, fat 4, fiber 2, carbs 8, protein 7

Cajun Breakfast Hash Browns

Preparation time: 10 minutes
Cooking time: 10 minutes
Servings: 2

Ingredients:
- 2 tablespoons olive oil
- 1 small onion, chopped
- 2 tablespoons garlic, minced
- 1 pound cauliflower, riced
- 1 teaspoon Cajun seasoning
- 8 ounces pastrami, shaved
- 2 tablespoons veggie stock
- 1 small green bell pepper, chopped

Directions:

Set your instant pot on sauté mode, add the oil and heat it up. Add onion, stir and cook for 2 minutes. Add garlic and cauliflower, stir and cook for 2 minutes more. Add pastrami, green bell pepper and Cajun seasoning, stir and cook for 2 minutes. Add stock, cover and cook on High for 4 minutes. Divide between plates and serve for breakfast. Enjoy!

Nutrition: calories 182, fat 4, fiber 2, carbs 4, protein 7

Eggs and Chives

Preparation time: 10 minutes
Cooking time: 2 minutes
Servings: 3

Ingredients:

- 3 tablespoons ghee
- 3 tablespoons cream cheese
- 3 eggs
- 1 tablespoon chives, chopped
- A pinch of salt and black pepper
- 1 cup water

Directions:

Divide grease 3 ramekins with the ghee and divide cream cheese in each. Crack an egg into each ramekin, season with a pinch of salt and black pepper and sprinkle chives on top. Add the water to your instant pot, add the steamer basket, add ramekins inside, cover and cook on High for 2 minutes. Serve hot. Enjoy!

Nutrition: calories 163, fat 4, fiber 2, carbs 7, protein 6

Eggs and Cheese Breakfast

Preparation time: 10 minutes
Cooking time: 16 minutes
Servings: 4

Ingredients:

- 2 cup cauliflower, riced
- 6 bacon slices, chopped
- 6 eggs
- ¼ cup coconut milk
- ½ cup cheddar cheese, shredded
- A pinch of salt and black pepper
- 1 small yellow onion, chopped
- 1 and ½ cups water

Directions:

Set your instant pot on sauté mode, add bacon, stir and cook for 2 minutes. Add onion, stir and cook for 2 minutes more. Add cauliflower rice, stir and cook for 2 minutes. In a bowl, mix eggs with cheese, salt, pepper, coconut milk and the veggie mix, stir everything and pour into a heatproof dish. Clean your instant pot, add the water and the trivet, add the baking dish inside, cover and cook on High for 10 minutes. Divide between plates and serve. Enjoy!

Nutrition: calories 182, fat 3, fiber 6, carbs 7, protein 7

Breakfast Blueberry Cake

Preparation time: 10 minutes
Cooking time: 30 minutes
Servings: 4

Ingredients:

- 2 cups coconut flour
- Zest from 1 lemon, grated
- 2 teaspoons baking powder
- ½ cup ghee
- ¾ cup stevia
- 1 teaspoon vanilla extract
- 1 egg
- ½ cup coconut milk
- 2/3 cup water
- 2 cups blueberries

Directions:

In a bowl, mix ghee with flour, baking powder, lemon zest and stevia and stir well. Add egg, vanilla and coconut milk and stir really well. Add blueberries, stir gently and pour into a cake pan. Add the water to your instant pot, add the steamer basket, add cake pan inside, cover pot and cook on Manual for 30 minutes. Divide between plates and serve for breakfast. Enjoy!

Nutrition: calories 172, fat 4, fiber 3, carbs 7, protein 7

Egg Casserole

Preparation time: 10 minutes
Cooking time: 25 minutes
Servings: 4

Ingredients:

- 2 cups water
- 1 yellow onion, chopped
- 1 and ½ cups ham, chopped
- 2 cups cheddar cheese, shredded
- 10 eggs
- 1 cup coconut milk
- A pinch of salt and black pepper
- A drizzle of olive oil

Directions:

Spray a baking dish with olive oil. In a bowl, mix onion with ham, cheese, eggs, coconut milk, salt and pepper and stir well. Pour this into the baking dish and spread evenly. Add the water to your instant pot, add the steamer basket, add the baking dish inside, cover and cook on Manual for 25 minutes. Slice, divide between plates and serve for breakfast. Enjoy!

Nutrition: calories 192, fat 4, fiber 2, carbs 6, protein 8

Breakfast Pancake

Preparation time: 10 minutes
Cooking time: 45 minutes
Servings: 4

Ingredients:

- 2 cups coconut flour
- 2 tablespoons stevia
- 2 eggs
- 2 teaspoons baking powder
- 1 and ½ cups coconut milk
- A drizzle of olive oil

Directions:

In a bowl, mix eggs with stevia and milk and whisk well. Add flour and baking powder and stir everything well again. Grease your instant pot with the oil, add the batter, spread into the pot, cover and cook on Low for 45 minutes. Slice pancake, divide between plates and serve for breakfast. Enjoy!

Nutrition: calories 182, fat 3, fiber 2, carbs 6, protein 8

Tomato and Spinach Eggs

Preparation time: 10 minutes
Cooking time: 20 minutes
Servings: 6

Ingredients:

- ½ cup coconut milk
- A pinch of salt and black pepper
- 12 eggs
- 3 cups spinach, chopped
- 1 cup tomato, chopped
- 3 green onions, chopped
- ¼ cup parmesan, grated
- 1 and ½ cups water
- A drizzle of olive oil

Directions:

In a bowl, mix eggs with salt, pepper, milk, green onion, spinach and tomato and stir well. Grease a baking dish with the olive oil, pour eggs mix, spread and sprinkle parmesan on top. Add the water to your instant pot, add the steamer basket, add baking dish inside, cover and cook on High for 20 minutes. Divide between plates and serve for breakfast. Enjoy!

Nutrition: calories 183, fat 4, fiber 4, carbs 7, protein 8

Breakfast Frittata

Preparation time: 10 minutes
Cooking time: 30 minutes
Servings: 4

Ingredients:
- 1 cup coconut cream
- 4 eggs
- 10 ounces canned green chilies
- A pinch of salt and black pepper
- ½ teaspoon cumin, ground
- 1 cup Mexican cheese, shredded
- ¼ cup cilantro, chopped
- 2 cups water

Directions:
In a bowl, mix eggs with coconut cream, salt, pepper, chilies, cumin and half of the cheese, stir well and pour this into a round pan. Add the water to your instant pot, add the trivet, place pan inside, cover and cook on High for 20 minutes. Spread the rest of the cheese and the cilantro over frittata, introduce in a preheated broiler for 5 minutes, slice and serve. Enjoy!

Nutrition: calories 254, fat 6, fiber 1, carbs 6, protein 14

Mexican Breakfast Casserole

Preparation time: 10 minutes
Cooking time: 25 minutes
Servings: 8

Ingredients:
- 1 pound sausage, ground
- 8 eggs, whisked
- 1 red bell pepper, chopped
- 1 red onion, chopped
- ½ cup green onions, chopped
- ½ cup coconut flour
- 1 cup cotija cheese, shredded
- 1 cup mozzarella cheese, shredded
- 1 tablespoon cilantro, chopped

Directions:
Set your instant pot on sauté mode, add sausage, stir and cook for 3 minutes. Add eggs, bell pepper, onion, green onions, coconut flour, cotija and mozzarella cheese, stir, cover and cook on High for 20 minutes. Add cilantro, stir your mix gently, divide between plates and serve for breakfast. Enjoy!

Nutrition: calories 265, fat 3, fiber 6, carbs 8, protein 8

Burrito Casserole

Preparation time: 10 minutes
Cooking time: 13 minutes
Servings: 6

Ingredients:
- 2 pound celeriac, peeled and cubed
- 4 eggs
- ¼ cup yellow onion, chopped
- 1 jalapeno, chopped
- 6 ounces ham, chopped
- A pinch of salt and black pepper
- ¼ teaspoon chili powder
- ¾ teaspoon taco seasoning
- Keto salsa for serving
- 1 cup water+ 1 tablespoon

Directions:

In a bowl, mix eggs with onion, jalapeno, celeriac, ham, salt, pepper, chili powder and taco seasoning and stir. Add 1 tablespoon water, stir again and pour everything into a casserole. Add the water to your instant pot, add the trivet, and casserole, cover pot and cook on Manual for 13 minutes. Divide between plates and serve for breakfast with some keto salsa on top. Enjoy!

Nutrition: calories 213, fat 4, fiber 6, carbs 7, protein 7

Breakfast Oatmeal

Preparation time: 10 minutes
Cooking time: 10 minutes
Servings: 2

Ingredients:
- ¼ cup chia seeds
- ¼ cup coconut, unsweetened and shredded
- 1/3 coconut, flaked
- 1/3 cup almonds, flaked
- ½ cup coconut milk
- 1 teaspoon vanilla extract
- 1 cup water
- 2 tablespoons swerve

Directions:

In your instant pot, mix coconut with almonds, coconut milk, vanilla, water and swerve, stir, cover and cook on High for 6 minutes. Add chia seeds, stir, cover the pot and leave it aside for 4 minutes more. Divide into bowls and serve for breakfast. Enjoy!

Nutrition: calories 173, fat 3, fiber 4, carbs 5, protein 6

Chocolate Oatmeal

Preparation time: 10 minutes
Cooking time: 10 minutes
Servings: 4

Ingredients:

- 1 cup coconut milk
- 2 and ½ tablespoon cocoa powder
- 4 cups water
- 2 cups coconut, shredded
- 1 teaspoon vanilla extract
- 1 teaspoon cinnamon powder
- 10 ounces cherries, pitted

Directions:

In your instant pot, mix coconut milk with water, cocoa powder, coconut, vanilla extract, cinnamon and cherries, stir, cover and cook on High for 10 minutes. Stir your chocolate oatmeal once again, divide into bowls and serve for breakfast. Enjoy!

Nutrition: calories 183, fat 4, fiber 2, carbs 5, protein 7

Blueberry and Yogurt Bowl

Preparation time: 10 minutes
Cooking time: 6 minutes
Servings: 1

Ingredients:

- 1/3 cup coconut milk
- 1/3 cup coconut, unsweetened and flaked
- 1/3 cup yogurt
- 1/3 cup blueberries
- 1 tablespoon chia seeds
- ½ teaspoon stevia
- ¼ teaspoon vanilla extract
- A sprinkle of cinnamon powder
- 1 and ½ cups water

Directions:

In a heatproof jar, mix coconut milk with coconut, yogurt, blueberries, chia, stevia, vanilla and cinnamon, stir well and cover with tin foil. Put the water in your instant pot, add the jar, cover and cook on High for 6 minutes. Transfer blueberry mix to a bowl and serve. Enjoy!

Nutrition: calories 152, fat 3, fiber 3, carbs 4, protein 6

Breakfast Cauliflower Pudding

Preparation time: 10 minutes
Cooking time: 10 minutes
Servings: 6

Ingredients:

- 2 cups coconut milk
- 1 and ¼ cups water
- 1 cup cauliflower rice
- ¾ cup coconut cream
- 2 tablespoons swerve
- 1 teaspoon vanilla extract

Directions:

In your instant pot, mix coconut milk with water, swerve and cauliflower rice, stir, cover and cook on High for 10 minutes. Add cream and vanilla extract, stir, divide into bowls and serve for breakfast. Enjoy!

Nutrition: calories 153, fat 3, fiber 2, carbs 6, protein 7

Scotch Eggs

Preparation time: 10 minutes
Cooking time: 12 minutes
Servings: 4

Ingredients:

- 1 pound sausage, ground
- 4 eggs
- 1 tablespoon olive oil
- 2 cups water

Directions:

Put 1 cup water in your instant pot, add the steamer basket, add eggs inside, cover, cook on High for 6 minutes, transfer eggs to a bowl filled with ice water, cool them down and peel. Divide sausage mix into 4 pieces, place them on a cutting board and flatten them. Divide eggs on sausage mix, wrap well and shape 4 balls. Add the oil to your instant pot, set on sauté mode, heat it up, add scotch eggs and brown them on all sides. Clean the pot, add 1 cup water, and the steamer basket, and scotch eggs inside, cover the pot and cook on High for 6 minutes. Serve them for breakfast. Enjoy!

Nutrition: calories 192, fat 4, fiber 2, carbs 4, protein 7

Celeriac and Bacon Breakfast

Preparation time: 10 minutes
Cooking time: 9 minutes
Servings: 6

Ingredients:

- 2 teaspoons parsley, dried
- 3 bacon strips
- 2 pounds celeriac, peeled and cubed
- 4 ounces cheddar cheese, shredded
- 1 teaspoon garlic powder
- A pinch of salt and black pepper
- 2 tablespoons water

Directions:

Set your instant pot on sauté mode, add bacon, stir and cook for a couple of minutes. Add garlic powder, salt, pepper, water and parsley and stir. Add celeriac, stir, cover and cook on Manual for 7 minutes. Divide between plates and serve for breakfast. Enjoy!

Nutrition: calories 164, fat 3, fiber 2, carbs 6, protein 7

Meat Quiche

Preparation time: 10 minutes
Cooking time: 30 minutes
Servings: 4

Ingredients:

- ½ cup coconut milk
- A pinch of salt and black pepper
- 6 eggs, whisked
- 4 bacon slices, cooked and crumbled
- 1 cup sausage, ground and cooked
- ½ cup ham, chopped
- 2 green onions, chopped
- 1 cup cheddar cheese, shredded
- 1 cup water

Directions:

In a bowl, mix eggs with salt, pepper, milk, sausage, bacon, ham, green onions and cheese and stir well. Pour this into a soufflé dish and spread. Add the water to your instant pot, add the trivet, add soufflé dish inside, cover pot and cook on High for 30 minutes. Serve hot for breakfast. Enjoy!

Nutrition: calories 200, fat 3, fiber 3, carbs 6, protein 6

Cinnamon Oatmeal

Preparation time: 10 minutes
Cooking time: 5 minutes
Servings: 2

Ingredients:

- 1 and ½ cups water
- ½ cup coconut, unsweetened and flaked
- ½ teaspoon cinnamon powder
- 2 apples, cored, peeled and chopped
- ¼ teaspoon ginger powder
- Stevia to the taste

Directions:

In your instant pot, mix water with coconut, cinnamon, apples, ginger and stevia to the taste, stir, cover and cook on High for 5 minutes. Stir again, divide into bowls and serve for breakfast. Enjoy!

Nutrition: calories 172, fat 4, fiber 2, carbs 6, protein 6

Cauliflower Congee

Preparation time: 10 minutes
Cooking time: 20 minutes
Servings: 4

Ingredients:

- 1 cup cauliflower rice
- 3 cups veggie stock
- 2 cups bok choy, chopped
- 2 tablespoons ginger, grated
- 2 cups shitake mushrooms, chopped
- 2 garlic cloves, minced
- 1 cup water
- 1 tablespoon coconut aminos

Directions:

In your instant pot, mix cauliflower rice with veggie stock, bok choy, mushrooms, garlic, water and aminos, stir, cover and cook on Manual for 20 minutes. Divide into bowls and serve for breakfast. Enjoy!

Nutrition: calories 183, fat 3, fiber 2, carbs 6, protein 3

Breakfast Avocado Cups

Preparation time: 10 minutes
Cooking time: 5 minutes
Servings: 4

Ingredients:

- 2 avocados, cut into halves and pitted
- 1 cup water
- A drizzle of olive oil
- 1 tablespoon chives, chopped
- A pinch of salt and black pepper
- 4 eggs

Directions:

Arrange all avocado cups on a cutting board and drizzle some olive oil over them. Crack an egg into each avocado cup, season with salt and pepper and sprinkle chives all over. Add the water to your instant pot, add the trivet, add avocado cups inside, cover and cook on High for 5 minutes. Divide avocado cups between plates and serve for breakfast. Enjoy!

Nutrition: calories 200, fat 3, fiber 3, carbs 7, protein 5

Smoked Salmon and Shrimp Breakfast

Preparation time: 10 minutes
Cooking time: 10 minutes
Servings: 4

Ingredients:

- 1 cup mushrooms, sliced
- 4 ounces salmon, smoked and chopped
- 4 ounces shrimp, deveined
- A pinch of salt and black pepper
- 4 bacon slices, chopped
- ½ cup coconut cream

Directions:

Set your instant pot on sauté mode, add bacon, stir and cook for 2 minutes, Add mushrooms, stir and cook for 1 minute more. Add salmon, shrimp, salt, pepper and coconut cream, stir, cover and cook on High for 5 minutes. Divide into bowls and serve for breakfast. Enjoy!

Nutrition: calories 180, fat 3, fiber 1, carbs 5, protein 8

Beef Breakfast Pie

Preparation time: 10 minutes
Cooking time: 30 minutes
Servings: 8

Ingredients:

- ½ onion, chopped
- 1 keto pie crust
- 1 small red bell pepper, chopped
- 1 pound beef, ground
- 8 eggs
- 1 and ½ cups water
- A pinch of salt and black pepper
- 1 tablespoon Italian seasoning
- A handful cilantro, chopped
- 1 teaspoon olive oil
- 1 teaspoon baking soda

Directions:

Set your instant pot on sauté mode, add the oil, heat it up, add beef, salt, pepper and Italian seasoning, stir and brown for 2 minutes. Add bell pepper and onion, stir and cook for 2 minutes more. Add baking soda and eggs, stir, cook for 3 minutes more and transfer to a bowl. Fill your piecrust with this mix and spread it well. Add the water to your instant pot, add the steamer basket, add pie inside, cover and cook on High for 20 minutes. Leave the pie to cool down, sprinkle cilantro on top, slice and serve for breakfast. Enjoy!

Nutrition: calories 258, fat 4, fiber 5, carbs 6, protein 5

Delicious Breakfast Skillet

It's going to be so tasty!

Preparation time: 10 minutes
Cooking time: 20 minutes
Servings: 4

Ingredients:

- 8 ounces mushrooms, chopped
- 2 tablespoons veggie stock
- A pinch of salt and black pepper
- 1 pound pork, minced
- 1 tablespoon olive oil
- ½ teaspoon garlic powder
- ½ teaspoon basil, dried
- 2 tablespoons Dijon mustard
- 2 zucchinis, chopped

Directions:

Set your instant pot on sauté mode, add oil, heat it up, add mushrooms, stir and sauté for 2 minutes. Add zucchini, salt, pepper, pork meat, garlic powder and basil, stir and cook for 3 minutes more. Add mustard and stock, stir, cover and cook on High for 15 minutes. Divide between plates and serve for breakfast. Enjoy!

Nutrition: calories 180, fat 5, fiber 2, carbs 5, protein 6

Pork Sausage Quiche

Preparation time: 10 minutes
Cooking time: 20 minutes
Servings: 5

Ingredients:
- 12 ounces pork sausage, chopped
- Salt and black pepper to the taste
- 2 teaspoons coconut cream
- 2 tablespoons parsley, chopped
- 10 mixed cherry tomatoes, halved
- 6 eggs
- 2 tablespoons parmesan, grated
- 2 cups water
- 5 eggplant slices

Directions:

Spread sausage pieces on the bottom of a baking dish and add eggplant and cherries over them. In a bowl, mix eggs with salt, pepper, parmesan, parsley and cream, whisk well and pour over sausage mixture. Add the water to your instant pot, add the steamer basket, add the baking dish inside, cover and cook on High for 20 minutes. Leave quiche to cool down a bit, slice and serve. Enjoy!

Nutrition: calories 240, fat 6, fiber 3, carbs 6, protein 7

Sausage, Leeks and Eggs Casserole

Preparation time: 10 minutes
Cooking time: 25 minutes
Servings: 4

Ingredients:
- 1 pound sausage, chopped
- ¼ cup coconut milk
- 4 asparagus stalks, chopped
- 1 leek, chopped
- 8 eggs, whisked
- 1 tablespoon dill, chopped
- A pinch of salt and black pepper
- ¼ teaspoon garlic powder
- 1 tablespoon olive oil
- 1 and ½ cups water

Directions:

Set your instant pot on sauté mode, add sausage, stir and brown for 3 minutes. Add asparagus and leek, stir and cook for 2 minutes more. In a bowl, mix eggs with garlic powder, salt, pepper, milk and dill and whisk well. Add sausage and veggie mix and stir. Drizzle the oil in a baking dish and add eggs and sausage mix. Add the water to your instant pot, add the trivet, add baking dish inside, cover and cook on High for 20 minutes. Slice, divide between plates and serve for breakfast. Enjoy!

Nutrition: calories 240, fat 5, fiber 3, carbs 5, protein 14

Almond Porridge

Preparation time: 5 minutes
Cooking time: 7 minutes
Servings: 2

Ingredients:

- 1 teaspoon cinnamon powder
- A pinch of nutmeg, ground
- A pinch of cloves, ground
- A pinch of cardamom, ground
- ½ cup almonds, ground
- 1 teaspoon stevia
- ¾ cup coconut cream

Directions:

In your instant pot, mix almonds with cream, stevia, cardamom, cloves, nutmeg and cinnamon, stir, cover and cook on High for 7 minutes. Divide into 2 bowls and serve for breakfast. Enjoy!

Nutrition: calories 163, fat 5, fiber 2, carbs 4, protein 8

Almond and Chia Breakfast

Preparation time: 5 minutes
Cooking time: 5 minutes
Servings: 2

Ingredients:

- 2 tablespoons almonds, chopped
- 1 tablespoon chia seeds
- 2 tablespoon pepitas, roasted
- 1/3 cup coconut milk
- 1/3 cup water
- A handful blueberries

Directions:

In your food processor, mix pepitas with almonds and pulse them well. In your instant pot, mix chia seeds with water and coconut milk and stir. Add pepitas mix, stir, cover pot and cook on High for 5 minutes. Add blueberries, toss a bit, divide into 2 bowls and serve for breakfast. Enjoy!

Nutrition: calories 150, fat 1, fiber 2, carbs 4, protein 2

Nuts Bowl

Preparation time: 5 minutes
Cooking time: 5 minutes
Servings: 1

Ingredients:

- 1 teaspoon pecans, chopped
- 1 teaspoon walnuts, chopped
- 1 teaspoon almonds, chopped
- 1 teaspoon pistachios, chopped
- 1 teaspoon pine nuts, chopped
- 1 teaspoon sunflower seeds
- 1 teaspoon stevia
- 1 teaspoon pepitas, raw
- 2 teaspoons raspberries
- 1 cup coconut milk

Directions:

In your instant pot, mix pecans with walnuts, almonds, pistachios, pine nuts, sunflower seeds, pepitas and stevia and stir. Add milk, stir, cover pot and cook on High for 5 minutes. Add raspberries, toss a bit, transfer to a bowl and serve for breakfast. Enjoy!

Nutrition: calories 100, fat 1, fiber 2, carbs 2, protein 4

Kale and Prosciutto Muffins

Preparation time: 10 minutes
Cooking time: 15 minutes
Servings: 4

Ingredients:

- ½ cup coconut milk
- 6 eggs
- 1 tablespoon olive oil
- Salt and black pepper to the taste
- ¼ cup kale, chopped
- 8 prosciutto slices
- ¼ cup chives, chopped
- 1 and ½ cups water

Directions:

In a bowl, mix eggs with milk, chives, salt, pepper and kale and whisk well. Grease a muffin tray with the oil, line with prosciutto slices and pour eggs and kale mix over them. Add the water to your instant pot, add the trivet, add muffin tray inside, cover pot and cook on High for 15 minutes. Leave muffins to cool down a bit, divide between plates and serve for breakfast. Enjoy!

Nutrition: calories 130, fat 1, fiber 1, carbs 2, protein 7

Bacon Muffins

Preparation time: 10 minutes
Cooking time: 20 minutes
Servings: 12

Ingredients:

- 1 cup bacon, chopped
- A pinch of salt and black pepper
- 1 and ½ cups water
- ½ cup ghee, melted
- 3 cups coconut flour
- 1 teaspoon baking soda
- 4 eggs
- 2 teaspoons lemon zest, grated

Directions:

In a bowl, mix flour with baking soda, eggs, lemon zest, ghee, salt, pepper and bacon, stir well and pour into a greased muffin tray. Add the water to your instant pot, add the trivet, add muffin tray inside, cover and cook on High for 20 minutes. Leave muffins to cool down a bit, divide between plates and serve them for breakfast. Enjoy!

Nutrition: calories 173, fat 3, fiber 2, carbs 5, protein 6

Cheddar and Parmesan Muffins

Preparation time: 10 minutes
Cooking time: 20 minutes
Servings: 6

Ingredients:

- 2 tablespoons olive oil
- 2 cups water
- 2 tablespoon parmesan, grated
- 1 cup cheddar cheese, grated
- 1 egg
- ½ teaspoon oregano, dried
- ¼ teaspoon baking soda
- 1 cup coconut flour
- A pinch of salt and black pepper
- ½ cup coconut milk

Directions:

In a bowl, mix flour with oregano, salt, pepper, parmesan, baking soda, milk, oil, egg and cheddar cheese, stir really well and pour into a greased muffin tray. Add the water to your instant pot, add the trivet, and the muffin tray inside, cover and cook on High for 15 minutes. Sprinkle parmesan over muffins, introduce them in a preheated broiler, broil for 5 minutes, divide them between plates and serve for breakfast. Enjoy!

Nutrition: calories 160, fat 1, fiber 2, carbs 3, protein 6

Eggs and Turkey

Preparation time: 10 minutes
Cooking time: 10 minutes
Servings: 4

Ingredients:
- 4 avocado slices
- A pinch of salt and black pepper
- 4 bacon slices, cooked
- 4 turkey breast slices, already cooked
- 2 tablespoons olive oil
- 4 eggs, whisked
- 2 tablespoons veggie stock

Directions:
Set your instant pot on sauté mode, add bacon, brown on both sides and transfer to a plate. Add the oil to your instant pot, heat it up, add eggs, salt, pepper and veggie stock, stir, cover and cook on High for 5 minutes. Divide turkey and bacon slices among 4 plates. Divide eggs and avocado slices as well and serve for breakfast. Enjoy!

Nutrition: calories 155, fat 2, fiber 2, carbs 4, protein 6

Chia Pudding

Preparation time: 2 minutes
Cooking time: 3 minutes
Servings: 4

Ingredients:
- ½ cup chia seeds
- 2 cups coconut milk
- ¼ cup almonds, chopped
- ¼ cup coconut, unsweetened and shredded
- 4 teaspoons stevia

Directions:
Put chia seeds in your instant pot, add milk, almonds, coconut and stevia, stir, cover and cook on High for 3 minutes. Divide into bowls and serve for breakfast. Enjoy!

Nutrition: calories 140, fat 1, fiber 1, carbs 2, protein 3

Pumpkin Spread

Preparation time: 10 minutes
Cooking time: 10 minutes
Servings: 4

Ingredients:

- 2 apples, peeled, cored and chopped
- 20 ounces pumpkin puree
- 1 tablespoon pumpkin pie spice
- 1 tablespoon stevia
- 10 ounces apple cider

Directions:

In your instant pot, mix apples with pumpkin puree, spice, stevia and cider, stir, cover, cook on High for 10 minutes, divide into jars and serve cold for breakfast. Enjoy!

Nutrition: calories 140, fat 3, fiber 1, carbs 3, protein 4

Mushroom, Tomatoes and Zucchini Mix

Preparation time: 10 minutes
Cooking time: 5 minutes
Servings: 5

Ingredients:

- 1 and ½ cups yellow onion, chopped
- 12 ounces mushrooms, chopped
- 15 ounces tomatoes, chopped
- 8 cups zucchini, sliced
- 1 tablespoon olive oil
- 2 garlic cloves, minced
- 1 basil sprigs, chopped
- A pinch of sea salt and black pepper

Directions:

Set your instant pot on sauté mode add the oil, heat it up, add garlic and onion, stir and cook for 2 minutes. Add salt, pepper, basil and mushrooms, stir and sauté for 30 seconds more. Add tomatoes and zucchini, stir, cover pot, cook on High for 3 minutes, divide between plates and serve for breakfast. Enjoy!

Nutrition: calories 136, fat 2, fiber 3, carbs 3, protein 4

Okra and Zucchinis Breakfast

Preparation time: 10 minutes
Cooking time: 10 minutes
Servings: 4

Ingredients:

- 1 and ½ cups red onion, roughly chopped
- 3 tablespoons olive oil
- 2 cups okra, sliced
- 1 cup mushrooms, sliced
- 1 cup cherry tomatoes, halved
- 1 cup water
- 2 cups zucchini, roughly chopped
- 2 cups yellow bell pepper, chopped
- Black pepper to the taste
- 2 tablespoons basil, chopped
- 1 tablespoon thyme, chopped
- ½ cup balsamic vinegar

Directions:

Put onion, tomatoes, okra, mushrooms, zucchini, bell pepper, basil, thyme, vinegar and oil in your instant pot and toss. Add black pepper, toss again well, also add the water, cover pot and cook on High for 10 minutes. Divide between plates and serve for breakfast. Enjoy!

Nutrition: calories 120, fat 2, fiber 2, carbs 3, protein 6

Squash and Cranberry Sauce

Preparation time: 10 minutes
Cooking time: 7 minutes
Servings: 4

Ingredients:

- ¼ cup raisins
- 2 acorn squash, peeled and roughly chopped
- 14 ounces cranberry sauce, unsweetened
- ¼ teaspoon cinnamon powder
- A pinch of sea salt and black pepper

Directions:

In your instant pot, mix squash with cranberry sauce, raisins, cinnamon, salt and pepper, stir, cover, cook on High for 7 minutes, divide into bowls and serve. Enjoy!

Nutrition: calories 140, fat 3, fiber 2, carbs 3, protein 4

Beef and Radish Hash

Preparation time: 10 minutes
Cooking time: 16 minutes
Servings: 2

Ingredients:
- 1 tablespoon olive oil
- 1 yellow onion, chopped
- 2 cups corned beef, cubed
- 2 garlic cloves, minced
- ½ cup beef stock
- A pinch of salt and black pepper
- 1 pound radishes, cut into quarters

Directions:

Set your instant pot on sauté mode, add oil, heat it up, add onion, stir and cook for 2 minutes. Add garlic and radishes, stir and sauté them for 4 minutes more. Add beef, stock, salt and pepper, stir, cover and cook on High for 10 minutes. Divide into bowls and serve for breakfast. Enjoy!

Nutrition: calories 160, fat 3, fiber 3, carbs 5, protein 4

Sweet Carrots Breakfast

Preparation time: 10 minutes
Cooking time: 4 minutes
Servings: 4

Ingredients:
- 1 and ½ cups coconut milk
- A pinch of cloves, ground
- A pinch of nutmeg, ground
- 1 small zucchini, grated
- 1 carrot, grated
- 2 tablespoons swerve
- ½ teaspoon cinnamon powder
- ¼ cup pecans, chopped

Directions:

In your instant pot, mix milk with cloves, nutmeg, zucchini, carrot, swerve, cinnamon and pecans, stir, cover and cook on High for 4 minutes. Divide into bowls and serve hot. Enjoy!

Nutrition: calories 100, fat 1, fiber 2, carbs 3, protein 4

Breakfast Omelet

Preparation time: 10 minutes
Cooking time: 10 minutes
Servings: 1

Ingredients:

- 1 ounces rotisserie chicken, shredded
- 1 teaspoon mustard
- 1 tablespoon homemade mayonnaise
- 1 tomato, chopped
- 2 bacon slices, cooked and crumbled
- 3 eggs, whisked
- 1 small avocado, pitted, peeled and chopped
- Salt and black pepper to the taste
- A drizzle of olive oil

Directions:

In a bowl, mix eggs with chicken, mustard, mayo, tomato, bacon, avocado, salt and pepper and whisk well. Set your instant pot on sauté mode, add the oil, heat it up, add eggs mix, spread and cook for 2 minutes. Cover your instant pot, cook your omelet on High for 2 minutes, divide it between plates and serve for breakfast. Enjoy!

Nutrition: calories 150, fat 2, fiber 6, carbs 8, protein 10

Nuts, Squash and Apples Breakfast

Preparation time: 10 minutes
Cooking time: 10 minutes
Servings: 4

Ingredients:

- ½ cup almonds, soaked for 12 hours and drained
- ½ cup walnuts, soaked for 12 hours and drained
- 2 apples, peeled, cored and cubed
- 1 butternut squash, peeled and cubed
- 1 teaspoon cinnamon powder
- 1 tablespoon stevia
- ½ teaspoon nutmeg, ground
- 1 cup coconut milk

Directions:

Put the almonds in your blender, pulse them well and transfer them to your instant pot. Add walnuts, apples, squash, cinnamon, stevia, milk and nutmeg, stir, cover and cook on High for 10 minutes. Divide into bowls and serve for breakfast. Enjoy!

Nutrition: calories 140, fat 1, fiber 2, carbs 6, protein 3

Leek and Beef Breakfast Mix

Preparation time: 10 minutes
Cooking time: 10 minutes
Servings: 4

Ingredients:

- 1 and 1/3 cups leek, chopped
- 1 cup kale, chopped
- ½ cup water
- 2 tablespoons olive oil
- 2 teaspoons garlic, minced
- 8 eggs
- 2/3 cup celeriac, peeled and grated
- 1 and ½ cups beef sausage, casings removed and chopped

Directions:

Set your instant pot on Sauté mode, add the oil, heat it up, add leeks, stir and sauté for 1 minutes. Add celeriac, kale, water and garlic, stir and sauté for 1 minute more. Add beef sausage and eggs, stir, cover and cook on High for 6 minutes. Divide this mix on plates and serve for breakfast. Enjoy!

Nutrition: calories 150, fat 2, fiber 2, carbs 5, protein 6

Strawberries and Coconut Breakfast

Preparation time: 10 minutes
Cooking time: 10 minutes
Servings: 2

Ingredients:

- 3 tablespoons coconut flakes, unsweetened
- 2 tablespoon strawberries, chopped
- 1 cup water
- 2/3 cup coconut milk
- ½ teaspoon stevia

Directions:

In your instant pot, mix strawberries with coconut flakes, water, milk and stevia, stir, cover and cook on High for 10 minutes. Divide into 2 bowls and serve for breakfast. Enjoy!

Nutrition: calories 110, fat 5, fiber 3, carbs 3, protein 3

Chorizo and Veggies Mix

Preparation time: 10 minutes
Cooking time: 15 minutes
Servings: 2

Ingredients:
- 1 pound chorizo, chopped
- 1 small yellow onion, chopped
- 2 garlic cloves, minced
- 4 bacon slices, chopped
- ½ cup beef stock
- 2 poblano peppers, chopped
- 1 cup kale, chopped
- 8 mushrooms, chopped
- ½ cup cilantro, chopped
- 1 avocado, peeled, pitted and chopped
- 4 eggs

Directions:

Set your instant pot on sauté mode, add chorizo and bacon, stir and cook for 2 minutes. Add garlic, onion and poblano peppers, stir and cook for 2 minutes more. Add kale, mushrooms and stock, stir, make 4 holes in this mix, crack an egg in each, cover pot and cook on High for 4 minutes. Divide this between plates, add avocado and cilantro on top and serve for breakfast. Enjoy!

Nutrition: calories 160, fat 5, fiber 3, carbs 5, protein 7

Delicious Vanilla and Espresso Oatmeal

Preparation time: 10 minutes
Cooking time: 10 minutes
Servings: 4

Ingredients:
- 1 cup coconut milk
- 1 cup coconut flakes
- 2 cups water
- 2 tablespoons stevia
- 1 teaspoon espresso powder
- 2 teaspoons vanilla extract
- Grated dark and bitter chocolate for serving

Directions:

In your instant pot, mix coconut flakes with water, stevia, milk and espresso powder, stir, cover and cook on High for 10 minutes. Add vanilla extract, stir, divide into bowls and serve with grated chocolate on top. Enjoy!

Nutrition: calories 172, fat 2, fiber 4, carbs 7, protein 8

Coconut and Pomegranate Oatmeal

Preparation time: 5 minutes
Cooking time: 2 minutes
Servings: 2

Ingredients:

- 1 cup coconut, shredded
- 1 cup water
- ¾ cup pomegranate juice
- Seeds from 1 pomegranate

Directions:

In your instant pot, mix coconut with water and pomegranate juice, stir, cover and cook on High for 2 minutes. Add pomegranate seeds, stir oatmeal, divide into bowls and serve for breakfast. Enjoy!

Nutrition: calories 183, fat 3, fiber 6, carbs 9, protein 6

Cauliflower Rice Bowl

Preparation time: 5 minutes
Cooking time: 7 minutes
Servings: 4

Ingredients:

- 1 cup cauliflower, riced
- ½ cup coconut chips
- 1 cup coconut milk
- 3 tablespoons stevia
- ¼ cup raisins
- ¼ cup almonds, chopped
- A pinch of cinnamon powder

Directions:

In your instant pot, mix cauliflower rice with coconut, coconut milk, stevia, raisins, almonds and cinnamon, stir, cover and cook on High for 7 minutes. Divide into bowls and serve for breakfast. Enjoy!

Nutrition: calories 172, fat 2, fiber 3, carbs 7, protein 10

Conclusion

The Ketogenic diet can really change your life! It will transform you into a healthy and happy person! It's one of the best diets ever! The best thing about this amazing lifestyle is that you don't have to make drastic changes. You only have to respect some simple rules and everything will be ok.

The purpose of this amazing cookbook you've discovered is to help you make the most delicious Ketogenic recipes ever using one of the most popular kitchen appliances: instant pots.

All the recipes are so easy to make at home and professionals in the field have tested them all.
So, what are you waiting for?
Get your instant pot and start your Ketogenic diet today!

Recipe Index

Made in the USA
San Bernardino, CA
30 November 2017